Access to Geography 1

Richard Kemp • Paul Carvin • Rebecca Mason

Second Edition

Oxford University Press

Acknowledgements

The publishers and authors would like to thank the following people for their permission to use copyright material:

Robert Aberman/Hutchinson Library p47; Aerofilms p68; Barnaby's Picture Library p7; G. Barone/Zefa p53 (top); Claus Benser/Zefa p80 (top left); Trygve Bolstad/ Panos Pictures p28,31; J. Allan Cash p37 (bottom), 46,58,69,76 (both), 80 (top right), 81 (top right); Celtic Picture Agency p54 (top left), 59,60; Richard N.G. Clements/Celtic Picture Agency p54 (top right); Lupe Cunha p83 (both), 85; Damm/Zefa p53 (middle); Helen Daykin p70 (right), 74 (both); Earth Satellite Corporation/Science Photo Library p50 (top right); Mark Edwards p81 (top left); Mary Evans Picture Library p8; Fiat Auto (UK) Ltd p41, 87; Figaro Magazine/Frank Spooner Pictures p45; GeoScience Features p49 (bottom), 50 (top left) 51; Ron Giling/Panos Pictures p24; Robert Harding p81; Hutchinson Library p64 (top); Michael Knights/ Froglets Publications Ltd p16; Roberto Koch/Agenzia Contrasto p38 (bottom left); R.P. Lawrence/Frank Lane p6 (right); A. Liesecke/Zefa p89; Nancy Durrell McKenna/Hutchinson Library p80 (bottom); Tony Morrison/South American Pictures p83 (bottom right); Brian Moser/Hutchinson Library p49 (top); R. Mulvaney/Science Photo Library p9 (top); Nick Oakes/Select p66 (bottom); Emery McLaren Orr p72 (lower top); Eligio Paoni/Agenzia Contrasto p44; Bernard Regent/Hutchinson Library p64 (bottom); Michael Rose/ Frank Lane p9 (bottom); M.J. Thomas/Celtic Picture Agency p62; Roger Tidman/Frank Lane p14 (main pic); Courtesy of United Nations p92; Guido Votano/ Panos Pictures p32; J. Watkins/Frank Lane p14 (top left), 66 (top); Janine Wiedel p72 (top); Wiltshire Newspapers p70; Zefa p37 (top), 38 (top right and bottom right); Courtesy of companies as shown p88.

Other photos have been provided by authors.

The cover photograph is reproduced by permission of Tony Stone Worldwide.

The Ordnance Survey map extracts on pages 55 and 63 are reproduced with the permission of the Controller of Her Majesty's Stationery Office © Crown copyright.

Every effort has been made to trace and contact copyright holders, but this has not always been possible. We apologise for any infringement of copyright.

The unit entitled 'Italy' was written by Alison Stevens.

Oxford University Press, Walton Street, Oxford OX2 6DP

Oxford New York Toronto
Delhi Bombay Calcutta Madras Karachi
Kuala Lumpur Singapore Hong Kong Tokyo
Nairobi Dar es Salaam Cape Town
Melbourne Auckland Madrid

and associated companies in
Berlin Ibadan

Oxford is a trade mark of Oxford University Press

© Oxford University Press 1991
First published 1991
Reprinted 1992 (twice)
Second Edition 1993

ISBN 0 19 833476 1

Typeset by The TypeFoundry, Northampton
Artwork by Hardlines Ltd, Charlbury, Oxon
Printed in Hong Kong

Introduction

Access to Geography has been carefully planned and written to meet the needs of the National Curriculum at Key Stage 3. The themes, topics, and case studies used in the three-book course are drawn from the National Curriculum programmes of study and are designed to cover all the appropriate statements of attainment.

The course has been planned as a practical response to the National Curriculum. The books have also been organised to match as much as possible the good practice geography teachers have developed in recent years. Each book is divided into half a dozen units, each based around a familiar unifying theme. Within each unit the material is organised in double-page spreads, the most practical format for classroom use.

The course is designed for students across a broad range of ability. The lively page design, the high quality visuals, the carefully-written text, and the range of student activities mean that the material is extremely accessible. Each book provides study material for a complete school year.

Differentiation

The books are designed to reflect the levels within Key Stage 3. Within the books each double-page spread contains a range of activities which allow students to work at their own level.

Geographical enquiry

Each book contains a variety of 'assignments' on double-page spreads. These are designed to encourage students in the development of their enquiry skills.

Regional case studies

Integrated within all the books are regional case studies. These exemplify and extend the material developing human, physical, and environmental themes and issues. Where appropriate, regional case studies are built on from one book to another.

Access to Geography is a practical and straightforward response to the needs of the National Curriculum.

CONTENTS

Rivers in the landscape

UK regional comparisons

Development

1 Weather in Britain

Figure 1 (below) The old village of Derwent was exposed when Howden Reservoir in Derbyshire dried up during a drought. (right) Clearing snow from a blocked road

Storm wreaks havoc, 13 dead

Scotland comes to a halt under white blanket

Hosepipe ban spreads

Figure 2 Newspaper headlines about the weather

Floods, storms, droughts, wet bank holidays, rain-disrupted sports fixtures or just unbroken sunshine. Not many days seem to go by without some aspect of the weather being in the headlines!

The weather is very much a part of the British way of life: we have hundreds of conversations about it every day; we forecast it continually on TV, radio, and in the newspapers; and we even like to blame it when things go wrong. Our language is full of sayings that are linked to the weather - have you ever felt 'under the weather'?

However, there is a very serious side to the effect that the weather and climate have on our lives, as the photos above show. On the night of 15 and 16 October 1987, 13 people were killed during a 'freak' storm (nicknamed 'Hurricane Mike') which swept across southern England. It left a trail of destruction behind it. Millions of pounds worth of damage was done to buildings, cars, and other structures. The collection of rare trees and plants at Kew Gardens was badly damaged. Hundreds of hectares of beautiful woodlands were destroyed, with trees snapped off as if they were match-sticks. It will be a lifetime before all of the damage is mended and everything restored to its former beauty.

In a similar way, other rare weather events or 'hazards' can disrupt our normal lives. Yet the effects of the weather are not just felt as a result of such rare hazards. The amount of crop or the yield that farmers will get from their land will depend upon the weather over a long period of time. For example, too little rain at a crucial time in the spring could cut the yield of a field of wheat by up to 50 per cent.

'Weather' is not the same as 'climate'

When you use the words 'weather' and 'climate', be careful! They do not mean the same thing. What you see out of the window now is what the weather is like today. But today's weather is different from yesterday's, and it will almost certainly be different again tomorrow. In Britain the weather is very variable - that's why we talk about it so much!

The climate of a place is the overall picture of what the weather tends to be like over a much longer period of time. Is this place generally warmer or colder than that place? How much rain could this place normally expect in a typical year?

Figure 3

Here is a typical weather map. On it you can see many of the different things that put together make up weather and climate.

PRECIPITATION
Mostly rain, but also other forms of moisture - snow, hail, dew, fog

TEMPERATURE
As measured in the shade

CLOUD
Amount and type of clouds

PRESSURE
The weight of the air in the atmosphere at a particular time and place

WIND
Wind speed and direction

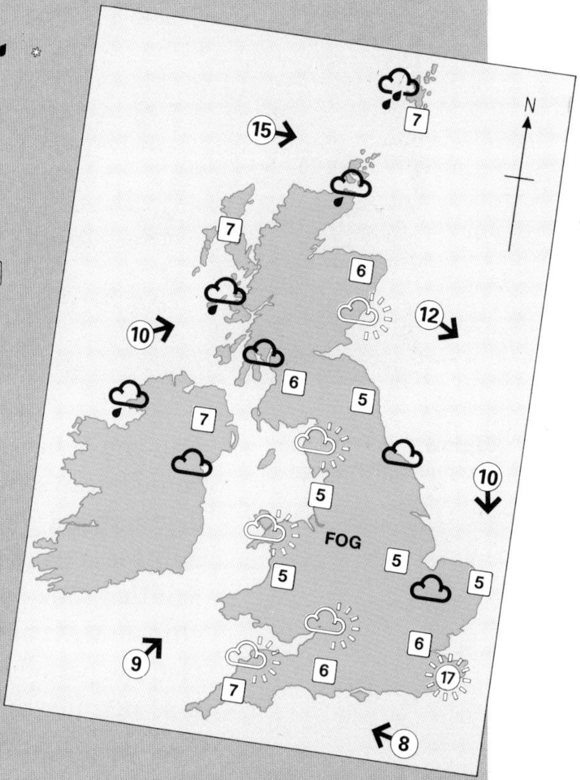

Figure 4

Activities

1 Working with a partner, make a list of as many sayings or expressions as you can think of that have a reference to the weather in them. Try to think how each one might have come about.

2 Choose one weather 'hazard'.
a) Make a list of all the ways in which it could affect people's lives.
b) Design a leaflet that could be given out to people if your hazard was forecast in their area. It should include information on what they should do to prepare for the hazard, and what they should do afterwards.

3 Hold a class discussion on the question 'How much does the weather affect the lives of people in Britain?' You should prepare for this individually before the discussion.

4 Research idea:
Keep a diary of 'weather reporting' for a week. Make a note of news items on TV or radio, or articles in the newspapers that have a link to the weather.

2 Patterns in the past

Figure 1 A Frost Fair on the River Thames

Can you believe that the River Thames could freeze so hard, and to such a depth, that a 'Frost Fair' could be held on it? It is true! Figure 1 shows a Frost Fair that took place in 1683-84. The climate was colder than it is today – in fact, the period between 1550 and 1850 is sometimes called the 'Little Ice Age'. A colder climate than today would have had many effects on people's lives, including the crops that they grew, their need for fuel and clothes to keep warm, and the illnesses from which they might have suffered.

In recent years, scientists (climatologists) have been able to build up a picture of the 'climatic change' that has taken place. Figure 2 shows the changes in temperature that have occurred during the last 200 000 years.

When the average July temperature fell below 10°C, Britain became so cold that much of it was covered with permanent snow and ice sheets – similar to those found in Antarctica today. These periods in history are called 'Ice Ages' or 'glacials'.

Colder temperatures in the past would also have had an impact on other aspects of the climate. For example, rainfall might have been heavier and more frequent; winds would have come from different directions; and mist and fog could have been more common. All of the water for the extra snow and ice would have come from the sea and as a result the level of the sea must have been lower than it is today. Experts believe that part of the English Channel was dry until about 10 000 years ago and that early Britons were able to walk from the continent. There was no need for a Channel tunnel!

In the same way that a detective uses a variety of different types of evidence (such as fingerprints) to solve a crime, climatologists have used evidence from many sources to piece together the picture of what the climate used to be like. Figure 3 explains these types of evidence and how they can be used in the study of past climates.

Figure 2 A graph showing temperature variations over the last 200 000 years

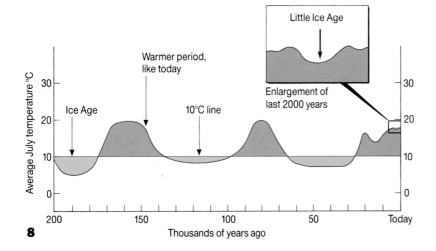

WHAT EVIDENCE DO WE HAVE THAT THE CLIMATE HAS CHANGED?

Ice boreholes

The ice sheet in Antarctica is over a kilometre thick. The ice has formed, layer by layer, each year over thousands of years. The way the ice layers formed tells scientists about how climate has changed.

Pollen analysis

Each type of plant has a different sort of pollen. The pollen of plants that grew thousands of years ago is sometimes preserved in peat bogs. Scientists can tell what sort of plants grew at the time, and thus what the climate was like.

Tree rings

Dendro-chronology is the proper word for the study of tree rings. Each ring in a tree trunk is one year's growth. The wider the ring the warmer the weather.

Old documents

The frost fair painting is just one type of documentary evidence for how climate has been different at various times in the past. Evidence also comes from books, diaries, and letters.

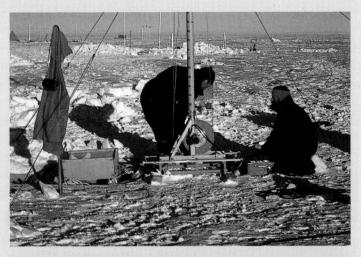

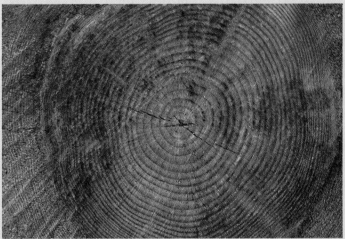

Figure 3 Types of evidence for climatic change

Activities

1 Study the picture of the Frost Fair in Figure l. In your own words, describe the scene as it would have been for a visitor to the fair in 1684. What sort of stalls were there? What sports were taking place?

2 Use the graph in Figure 2 to find out when the last Ice Age started and when it finished.

3 How much of the last 200 000 years has been Ice Age? Work out your answer as a percentage.

4 Research idea:
Try your own hand at 'dendro-chronology'. Find a recently cut down tree and measure the thickness of the tree rings. Draw a chart to show this information. Can you spot any patterns?

3 Patterns across the country

Britain is a country of marked contrasts in its weather and climate. Differences exist between the east and the west, the north and the south, the centre and the coasts, not to mention the highlands and the lowlands. People have adapted to these differences in many ways, including the way in which the land is farmed. This has affected the appearance of the landscape, and even the ways in which people live their lives from one day to the next. It is possible to find patterns in Britain's climate, and Figure 3 explains why they occur. However, don't be misled into believing some popular myths about the climate! For example, it doesn't really rain every day in Manchester as many people would have us believe!

Figure 1 Some information about the climate of the British Isles

'We run a small hotel in South Devon. Devon is sometimes called the 'English Riviera' as the weather is so mild. There are few frosts in winter, and we even have a palm tree growing in the garden. There are lots of market gardens around here, as things ripen earlier here than anywhere else in Britain. Mind you, it does seem to rain a lot, but don't tell the tourists!'

'I farm in Norfolk, and grow cereal crops like wheat and barley, and some oil seed rape. The land is flat, the soil fertile, but the main reason for growing cereals is the climate. The warm summers, with high amounts of sunshine, are what cereal crops need. Rainfall is just about adequate, although because our rainfall is the lowest in Britain, we do spray irrigate at times.'

'I'm an executive with an oil company based at Aberdeen. This can be a pretty cold place to live, especially when the wind is blowing in off the North Sea. And when I go out to the rigs, it can be pretty stormy out there. There is not as much snow here as in the nearby mountains, as this is lower ground and near the sea.'

'I'm a ranger in the Snowdonia National Park. What I notice most is the amount of rain, especially on the mountains. On the highest ground much of the precipitation falls as snow, which can lie on the ground for up to six months. Apart from tourism, most of the land is used for forestry and sheep farming.'

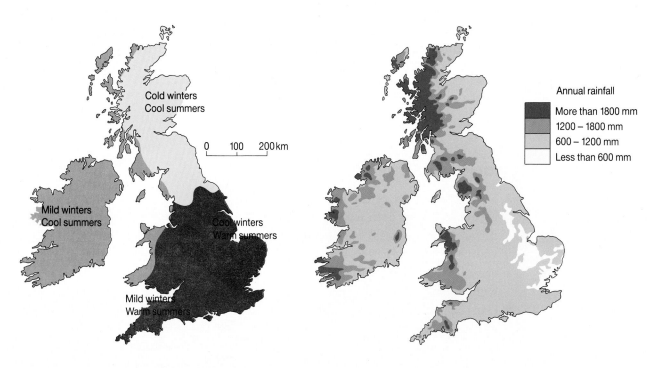

Cold winters
Cool summers

Mild winters
Cool summers

Cool winters
Warm summers

Mild winters
Warm summers

0 100 200 km

Annual rainfall

More than 1800 mm
1200 – 1800 mm
600 – 1200 mm
Less than 600 mm

(a) The effect of latitude (distance North or South of the equator) on our climate

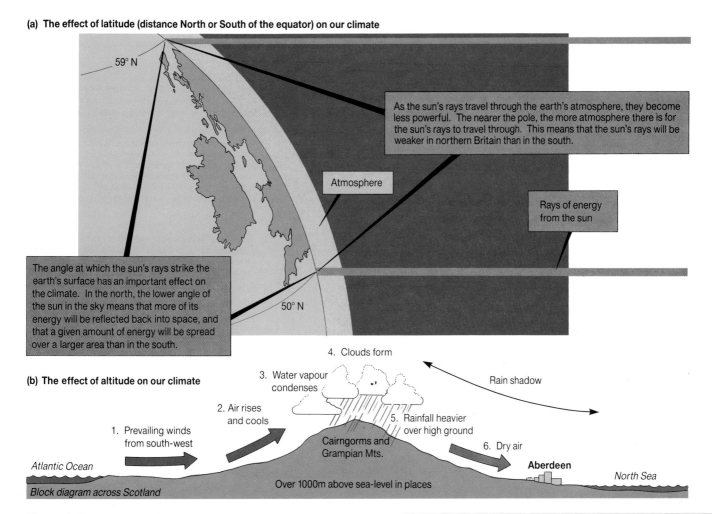

59° N

As the sun's rays travel through the earth's atmosphere, they become less powerful. The nearer the pole, the more atmosphere there is for the sun's rays to travel through. This means that the sun's rays will be weaker in northern Britain than in the south.

Atmosphere

Rays of energy from the sun

The angle at which the sun's rays strike the earth's surface has an important effect on the climate. In the north, the lower angle of the sun in the sky means that more of its energy will be reflected back into space, and that a given amount of energy will be spread over a larger area than in the south.

50° N

(b) The effect of altitude on our climate

4. Clouds form

3. Water vapour condenses

Rain shadow

2. Air rises and cools

1. Prevailing winds from south-west

5. Rainfall heavier over high ground

6. Dry air

Atlantic Ocean

Cairngorms and Grampian Mts.

Aberdeen

North Sea

Block diagram across Scotland

Over 1000m above sea-level in places

Figure 2 Two important factors which influence weather and climate in Britain

Table for Activities 2 and 3

Location	Annual rainfall mm	Mean July temperature °C	Mean January temperature °C	Ways in which climate affects people's lives	Some reasons for the climate
1	2	3	4	5	6
South Devon					
Norfolk					
Aberdeen					
Snowdonia					

Activities

1 The people talking in Figure 1 have explained how they view the climate in their area. Write a similar personal account for the part of the country in which you live.

2 Make a large copy of the table (below left). Using the information in Figure 1 and an atlas to help you, fill in columns 2-5 with more detailed data of how climate varies from one part of the country to another. The three rows at the bottom are for your choice of location to complete the coverage of Britain.

3 Make use of Figure 2 to help you fill in some details that help to explain the climate in different parts of the country. Use column 6 of the table to write in your answer.

4 *Recording the weather*

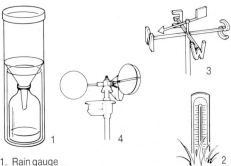
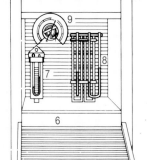
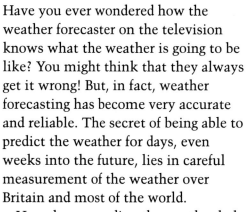
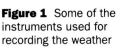

1. **Rain gauge**
   This is used to measure the depth of rain in millimetres that falls on the ground. Modern technology has given us some rain gauges that will send the rainfall information to a central computer.

2. **Soil thermometer**
   A thermometer stuck into the ground is useful as it gives the temperature from a plant's point of view. If the soil temperature falls too low plants will not grow. If there is a frost they might die or be badly damaged.

3. **Wind direction**
   The wind vane turns freely in the wind and will face the direction from which the wind is blowing.

4. **Anemometer**
   This revolves in the wind. The faster the wind speed, the faster it revolves. By counting the revolutions it is possible to calculate the wind speed.

5. **Sunshine recorder**
   The glass ball focuses direct sunlight onto a revolving paper disc, where it burns a mark. If the sun isn't shining, no mark is made.

6. **Stevenson Screen**
   This houses other instruments, but is not an instrument itself. Air can move freely through the slats of the screen, the white colour reflects the worst of the heat, and the roof keeps the rain out! All this gives a place where 'true' temperature readings can be obtained.

7. **Maximum/Minimum thermometer**
   This is a modified thermometer that can record both the maximum and minimum temperatures that have been reached during a 24 hour period. It can then be reset to do the job again.

8. **Wet/dry bulb thermometer**
   This is used to measure the water content or humidity of the air.

9. **Barometer**
   Barometers work by measuring the 'weight' of the air above them. Sometimes atmospheric pressure is measured in millibars (mb), 1000 mb is 'average' pressure. A figure above this is 'high' pressure and usually gives dry, calm and stable weather. 'Low' pressure is below 1000 mb and usually indicates wet or changeable weather.

Figure 1 Some of the instruments used for recording the weather

Have you ever wondered how the weather forecaster on the television knows what the weather is going to be like? You might think that they always get it wrong! But, in fact, weather forecasting has become very accurate and reliable. The secret of being able to predict the weather for days, even weeks into the future, lies in careful measurement of the weather over Britain and most of the world.

How does recording the weather help us to forecast what the weather is going to be like tomorrow? The weather is brought to a particular place by the wind. If we know what the weather is like where the wind is coming from, it is reasonably easy to predict what the weather will be like. So, if the wind is blowing from the west and it's raining in Ireland today, you could be fairly certain that it will rain in England tomorrow. Figure l shows the type of equipment forecasters use to make these accurate weather records.

How can we make long-range weather forecasts? Farmers and other people need to know what the weather is going to be like for a week or more in advance. Weather forecasters use the information that they have gathered over many years to make these long-range forecasts. In fact, accurate weather records exist for almost 100 years for the entire country. The weather tends to follow certain trends or patterns. If the pattern of weather in the last week is very similar to a pattern that happened in past years, there is a good chance that the weather for the next week will be like the past as well. All the weather records are now on computer, so it does not take too long to check all of them.

Satellites are used increasingly for recording and forecasting the weather. You will probably have seen moving satellite pictures of the weather on TV, and these enable scientists to watch the weather as it changes from day to day.

It is very important that you site your weather recording instruments carefully, away from trees or buildings.

Temperature

You may have a thermometer at home. Make sure that it is not in direct sunlight. Always take the temperature at the same time of day.

Rainfall

You can easily make your own rain gauge as shown in this diagram (right).

Wind

Most churches have a wind vane to tell you where the wind is coming from, or you could try making one. You could use the Beaufort Scale to measure wind speed. This describes the wind's strength by the effect it has on things like trees.

The Beaufort Scale

Nº	Name (speed, mph)	Effects
0	Calm (0)	Smoke rises vertically
1	Light air (1-3)	Smoke drifts
2	Light breeze (4-7)	Leaves rustle, vane moves
3	Gentle breeze (8-12)	Leaves and twigs move
4	Moderate breeze (13-18)	Small branches move
5	Fresh breeze (19-24)	Small trees sway
6	Strong breeze (25-31)	Large branches move
7	Moderate gale (32-38)	Large trees sway
8	Gale (39-46)	Twigs break off trees
9	Strong gale (47-54)	Large branches come down
10	Whole gale (55-63)	Trees uprooted
11	Storm (64-72)	Widespread general damage
12	Hurricane (73-82)	Widespread devastation

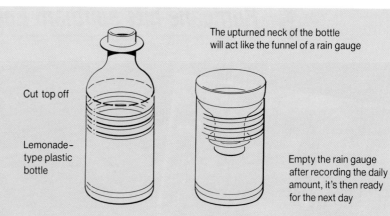

Cut top off

Lemonade-type plastic bottle

The upturned neck of the bottle will act like the funnel of a rain gauge

Empty the rain gauge after recording the daily amount, it's then ready for the next day

Figure 2 (above) Making your own weather station. The Beaufort Scale was written in 1805 by Admiral Sir Francis Beaufort and has been updated several times since then

Figure 3 (above right) A local weather forecast from the *Eastern Daily Press*, 21 July 1990

Eastern Daily Press   21st July 1990

Forecast for lunchtime today

King's Lynn · 26 · ☀ · 23
Cromer · 10 · 15
Norwich · Yarmouth
5 · 27 · 10
Thetford · ☀ · Lowestoft

Sunny · Fine · Fair · Cloudy/Dull · Rain

Thunder · Snow · Hail · Deg. C (18) · Mph (20)

Smooth · Slight · Moderate · Rough

General situation – High pressure continues to dominate the weather over the British Isles.

East Anglia – Today will be another fine and dry day, with long sunny spells for most of the time, although there will be rather more cloud around later in the day. Temperatures will reach 28 C in most inland areas, (82 F) and a degree or so lower than yesterday. Winds will be light, but more generally from the east.

North Sea – Wind light, occasionally moderate, easterly. Fair. Visibility good. Sea slight.

Outlook – Warm and dry with sunny spells.

METEOROLOGICAL OBSERVATIONS AT MORLEY
(Taken at 10.00 BST)

1990	Bar.	Max.	Min.	Grass	Sun	Rain
	In/mb	Deg.	Deg.	Deg.	Hrs.	Min.
July 18	30.42 (1030)	25.8	5.8	3.1	14.1	0.0
July 19	30.33 (1027)	29.2	9.0	5.9	13.5	0.0
July 20	30.27 (1025)	—	11.8	8.7	—	—

Rainfall for month to date 22.3
Mean rainfall for June 53.5

J. G. HILTON, Observer.
Morley Research Centre

Activities

1 Figure 3 is some weather information taken from a local daily paper. The map uses symbols to show what conditions are like. Use symbols to show what your local weather map would be like today.

2 In your own words, explain why having accurate weather forecasts can be very useful to different people.

3 Detailed observations from Morley are given in Figure 3.
   a) What was the daily range of temperature for 18 July?

   b) What might account for the much higher minimum temperature on 20 July than on 18 July?

4 Research idea:
   a) Keep a record of the 'predicted' weather for a week from TV, radio, or newspapers.
   b) Keep your own weather recordings for the same period.
   c) Compare the two sets of results. Try to explain any differences.

5 Hurricane hits southern England

Figure 1 Damage to trees and property caused by the hurricane of 16 October 1987

Look at the photographs of the sort of damage caused by the hurricane that swept across southern England during the night of 15-16 October 1987. Try to imagine what it must have been like both when it was happening and during the chaos that followed.

The hurricane started life as an area of low pressure, a depression, out in the Atlantic Ocean. As the depression moved towards Britain the atmospheric pressure got lower and lower and the winds got faster and faster. The map shows how the centre of the hurricane moved north-eastwards, leaving a trail of destruction behind it. Thirteen people lost their lives as a result of the tremendous winds and many more were seriously injured. Thousands of homes were damaged, and it was weeks before everything returned to normal.

Figure 3 shows the wind speeds that were recorded at Shoeburyness in Essex during that fateful night. By definition, hurricane-force wind is over 120km/hour. So in many places the storm was not strictly speaking a hurricane. Real hurricanes normally occur much nearer the equator, where the higher temperatures provide them with huge amounts of energy to do terrible destruction and damage.

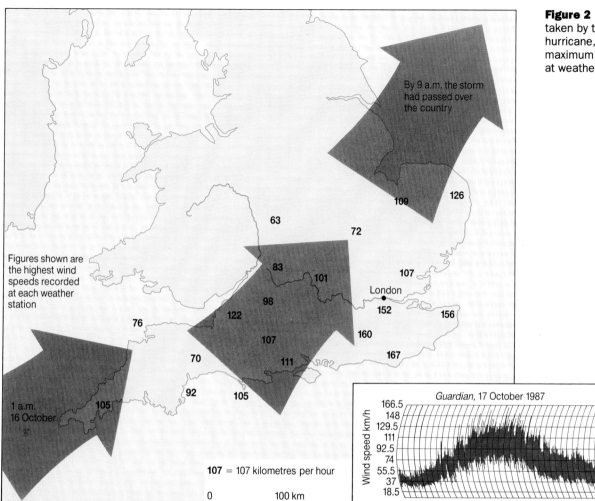

Figure 2 The path taken by the hurricane, with maximum wind speeds at weather stations

By 9 a.m. the storm had passed over the country

Figures shown are the highest wind speeds recorded at each weather station

1 a.m. 16 October

London

109   126

63

72

83   101

107

98

152   156

122   160

76   107   167

70   111

92   105

107 = 107 kilometres per hour

0   100 km

Guardian, 17 October 1987

Wind speed km/h

166.5
148
129.5
111
92.5
74
55.5
37
18.5

Time GMT   01   02   03   04   05   06   07   08   09   10   11

Figure 3 The anemogram or wind speed record from the Shoeburyness weather station in Essex

Activities

1 Imagine that you were living in an area that was hit by the hurricane. Write an account of what happened, using your own home as the scene for the story. Describe:
a) what you were thinking when the hurricane was at its worst;
b) the scene that met you when you went outside in the morning.

2 How different might things have been if the hurricane had occurred during the day rather than at night?

3 Draw your own map to show some features of the hurricane, including:
a) where it started;
b) the path that it took;
c) the areas of highest wind speed.

4 Research idea:
Use your school library and other books to find out more about hurricanes. In particular, try to discover the answer to these questions:
a) Which areas of the world are affected by hurricanes?
b) What are the local names for hurricanes?
c) What are the characteristics of a true hurricane?
d) How do the events of 15-16 October 1987 compare with what takes place during a true hurricane?

6 Assignment: The 1987 hurricane

... Friday 16th October 1987 7 a.m. ...

... HURRICANE HITS SE ENGLAND ...

... AREAS DEVASTATED ...

... DAMAGE ESTIMATED £ MILLIONS ...

Background information

This was the telex message flashed into the offices of the *Kent and Sussex Gazette*. Immediately, a team of reporters was sent to Brasted Chart in Kent, one of the worst-hit areas. Their job was to get eyewitness accounts of the hurricane and its aftermath.

Your assignment

Work in pairs or on your own.
You are the editor of the *Kent and Sussex Gazette*. Look at all the information given here, which has been sent back by your team of reporters. Your paper is going to publish a special hurricane edition, to show:

- the devastation caused by the hurricane;
- the effects that it has had on people's lives;
- the scale of the clear-up operation.

Figure 1 Storm damage in the Brasted Chart area of Kent

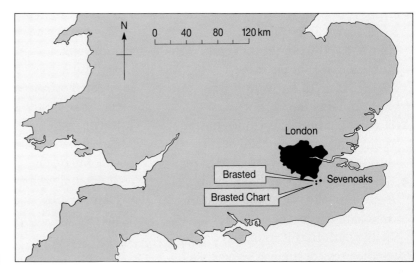

Figure 2 The location of Brasted Chart

I live on the Chart, the name given to the wooded area above the village. The storm woke us all up at 3 o'clock in the morning. My daughter was really frightened - we spent the rest of the night huddled together downstairs. All the trees in the garden have been blown down - it looks a real mess. We've no phone or electricity. All the food in the freezer is ruined. The only light we've got is from candles and we cook on the coal fire in the sitting room.
Hilary Kerr

My shop in the village has run out of all sorts of things - things like candles, gas, and convenience foods - as people try to cope with the aftermath of the hurricane.
Vera Harris

It's lucky that there's an army depot a few miles away. The local council just don't have the type of equipment needed to move all the trees that are blocking the roads. One 50metre stretch had 37 trees blocking it! We've sent a request to the forestry commission in Scotland to send us some more chain saws!
Corporal Nigel Smith

I was coming home from work on the late shift. Trees seemed to be falling down all around me. I decided to get out and walk! A few seconds later a huge tree fell on the rear of my car. I think it's totally ruined - I'm waiting for the lady from my insurance company. Mind you, I'm lucky to be alive!
Derek Mason

I work for the Northern Ireland Electricity Board. I've been flown over here with a team of engineers to help to mend the electricity cables - the local engineers just couldn't cope, there's so much damage! I reckon it will be several weeks before everybody has their power back, so we've just taken an emergency generator to the old people's home up the road.
Patrick Docherty

I run the pub on the Chart. It wasn't damaged, but my trade will be. Nobody can get to the pub for a drink - nor can the brewery get through to deliver any more beer.
Bob Owen

The National Trust bought its first piece of land at Toys Hill at the top of Brasted Chart. It was a beautiful area of beech woodland. Today it looks as though a war has been fought on it - trees have been uprooted, or snapped off as if made of matchsticks. A lifetime's work has been ruined. It could take hundreds of years to get back to its former glory.
Maureen Field

Half-term has come early to my school! Trees fell onto the roof in the night and it can't open until it's mended. I'm not allowed to play in the woods though, the army men have said it's too dangerous - a tree might fall on me!
Amy Kerr

Work Programme A

Read all the information carefully, and then write down some notes in answer to these questions:

- What are some of the ways in which the hurricane affected the area and the people who live there?
- How were lives in danger
  a) during the hurricane?
  b) afterwards?
- What slowed down the attempts to get life back to normal after the hurricane?

Work Programme B

As editor, you must design the front page of the special hurricane edition. It has to give the reader a feel of what is in the rest of the paper. You should use the initial eye-witness accounts from your team of reporters to help you – you will give them the job of writing full accounts when they return.

There are a number of things you must think about:

- The layout of the front page is very important. Try looking at actual newspapers to help you. Make a rough draft first.
- The headlines must have an impact, but also should be short and to the point.
- What about photographs and/or illustrations? A photographer will be sent to the area to take photographs for your approval.
- To have maximum impact, the articles should be quite short and they should keep to the facts.

1 *The essential liquid*

How much water do you think you use in your home every day? The average household uses about half a tonne. It is used in lots of ways – for baths and showers, for cooking and drinking, for washing and cleaning, for watering the garden. Water is an essential part of our day-to-day life. Living in Britain, we would find it difficult to manage without a reliable supply of clean water delivered directly to our homes.

Water is also essential in the making of many products, both in farming and industry. The quantities of water used by British industry are huge, twice as much as is used in all our homes. Figure 2 shows how much water is used in the making of just a few products.

Water used in the making of food products has to be very clean, but much of the water used in factories and on farms does not need to be as pure and clean as the water that is piped into our homes. The largest use of water in industry is for cooling things down, as in power stations. Some of the water used by industry becomes contaminated by chemicals or other dangerous (poisonous or 'toxic') substances. Such water has to be carefully treated before it can be allowed to enter the natural water.

At home, when you turn on the tap you expect the water coming out to be clean and fresh, and pure enough to drink. But is our water always safe? The headlines in Figure 3 and the account of what happened at Camelford (Figure 4) show that it is not always the case.

HOW YOU USE IT	AVERAGE AMOUNTS	×	TOTAL NUMBER PER DAY	=	TOTAL
Taking a bath	90 litres	×		=	
Taking a shower	27 litres	×		=	
Flushing a toilet	9 litres	×		=	
Washing face/hands	9 litres	×		=	
Getting a drink	1 litre	×		=	
Brushing teeth	1 litre	×		=	
Washing clothes	118 litres per load	×		=	
Watering the garden with a sprinkler	9 litres per minute	×		=	
Other	*You estimate!*	×		=	
				TOTAL	

Figure 1 How water is used in the home

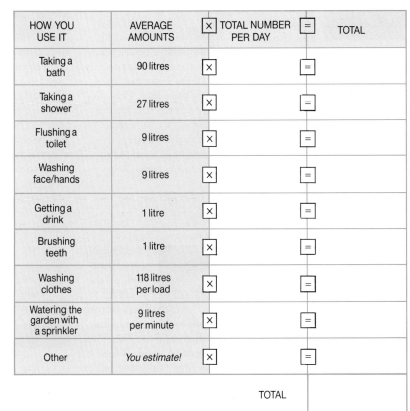
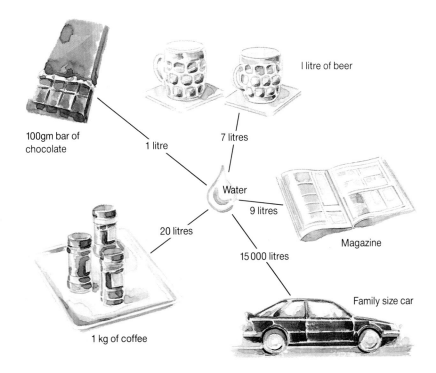

100gm bar of chocolate — 1 litre

1 litre of beer — 7 litres

Water

Magazine — 9 litres

Family size car — 15 000 litres

1 kg of coffee — 20 litres

Figure 2 How water is used in industry

400 towns drink 'dirty' water

Battle to clean Britain's dirty rivers 'is being lost'

Britain's troubled waters

Camelford authority pollutes Devon river

Figure 3 Newspaper headlines

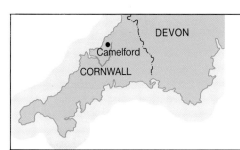

Something in the water

On 7th July 1988, the South-West Water Authority was responsible for the contamination of water in the town of Camelford and the surrounding villages. Twenty tonnes of aluminium sulphate was dumped accidentally into the Lowermoss Treatment Plant, resulting in the poisoning of water supplies to 20 000 people.

Figure 4

WHAT THE LOCALS SAID ABOUT THE CAMELFORD 'ACCIDENT'

"The day after I started suffering from stomach cramps, muscle pains, and continual diarrhoea."
- John Mapstone, local resident

"Customers kept arriving complaining about their hair turning green."
- Joanne Jeffs, hairdresser

"When I ran a bath the water was blue!"
- Rachel Tyler, local resident

"Within 48 hours, after drinking a cup of tea, huge blisters appeared all over the gums under my upper lip. I haven't been able to play the flute since and so I've lost my job."
- Tim Wheater, musician

"The fishing in the River Camel was ruined, 60 000 fish were killed by the poison."
- John Saunders, local anglers association

"Within a week 1300 of my chickens had died."
- Ray Smith, farmer

"Every time I made a cup of tea or coffee the milk curdled, and it tasted disgusting."
- Anna Clark, local resident

Figure 5

Activities

1 Work out how much water your family uses in a day. Do this by making your own copy of Figure l, and filling in the amounts. The figures given may seem a bit high, but people often leave the tap running for longer than they think.

2 Compare your family's use of water with other members of the class. Draw a bar graph to show how much water is used by ten different families.

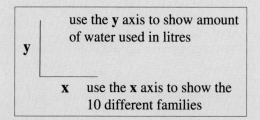

3 How could you and your family save on your use of water? Try and list at least five ways you might use less water.

4 Study the information about the Camelford 'accident' in Figures 4 and 5. Using this information, and your own ideas, produce *either* a newspaper report for the local South-West Daily *or* a short radio news item for the local radio station. In your report you will want to include something about what caused the accident, and what the effects of it were. Also include interviews with local people about their experiences and their views on what happened.

2 Where does our water come from?

Figure 1 The life cycle of a drop of water

It is an amazing fact that the oceans hold 97 per cent of all the world's water. A further 2 per cent is frozen in the polar ice caps. That leaves just 1 per cent to provide all the water we use, as well as the water in all the lakes and rivers in the world, all the water in the atmosphere, and all the water in the ground. With only 1 per cent of the world's water available to meet our needs, that water has to be constantly recycled.

The story of how this 1 per cent of water is recycled is not a simple one. In Figure 1, Walter Droplet describes his journey through the natural water cycle. Water in the cycle is never used up, it just goes round and round. That is why it is called the water, or hydrological, cycle.

The hydrological cycle is one form of natural system. Figure 2 is a basic diagram of a system at work. Notice that in any system there are three questions that we need to explore.

Figure 2 A simple system

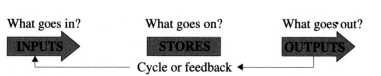

Activities

1 Experiment idea:
You can make your own hydrological cycle by carrying out a simple experiment. How you do this is explained in Figure 3. You will need a kettle, two cups, and some water.

2 Using the information in the cartoon about Walter Droplet, copy and complete the diagram of a hydrological cycle (Figure 4) and the summary table (Figure 5).

Method: 1. Half fill the kettle with water and switch on. When the water starts to boil, steam will come out of the spout. Hold one cup above the spout so that the steam hits it. 2. When the steam hits the cold surface of the cup, it will condense into water. Let the water drip out of the cup you are holding into the second cup. 3. Complete the cycle by pouring the water back into the kettle.

Figure 3 A do-it-yourself hydrological cycle

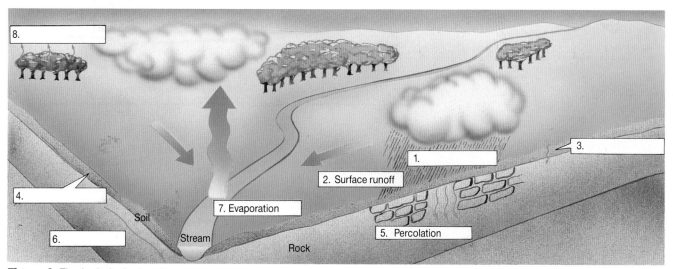

Figure 4 The hydrological cycle

Key Word	Definition
1. _ _ _ _ _	Rain, snow, sleet, hail, frost: moisture in the atmosphere.
2. Surface runoff	_ _ _ _ _ _ _ _ _ _ _ _ _ _ _ _ _ _ _
3. _ _ _ _ _	Gradual movement of water into soil.
4. _ _ _ _ _	Movement of water through the soil towards the stream.
5. Percolation	_ _
6. _ _ _ _ _ _ _ _ _	Movement of water through the rock towards the stream.
7. Evaporation	_ _ _ _ _ _ _ _ _ _ _ _ _ _ _ _ _ _
8. _ _ _ _ _	The loss of moisture by plants through their stomata (pores).

Figure 5 For use with Activity 2

You know how water is recycled in the natural system. But how does that water eventually reach our homes? This is where people step in. The diagram on the right shows you how we get the water we can drink. Follow it carefully through the four stages.

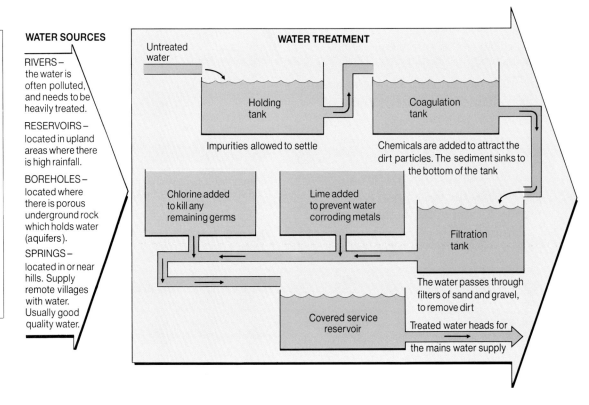

WATER SOURCES

RIVERS – the water is often polluted, and needs to be heavily treated.

RESERVOIRS – located in upland areas where there is high rainfall.

BOREHOLES – located where there is porous underground rock which holds water (aquifers).

SPRINGS – located in or near hills. Supply remote villages with water. Usually good quality water.

WATER TREATMENT

Untreated water

Holding tank

Impurities allowed to settle

Coagulation tank

Chemicals are added to attract the dirt particles. The sediment sinks to the bottom of the tank

Chlorine added to kill any remaining germs

Lime added to prevent water corroding metals

Filtration tank

The water passes through filters of sand and gravel, to remove dirt

Covered service reservoir

Treated water heads for the mains water supply

Figure 6 The human water cycle

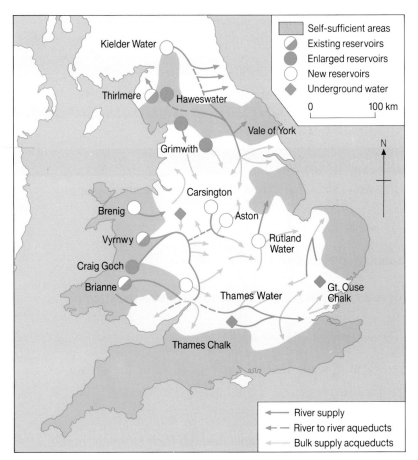

Figure 7 The major reservoirs of England and Wales

Self-sufficient areas
Existing reservoirs
Enlarged reservoirs
New reservoirs
Underground water

0   100 km

N

Kielder Water
Thirlmere
Haweswater
Vale of York
Grimwith
Carsington
Brenig
Aston
Vyrnwy
Rutland Water
Craig Goch
Brianne
Thames Water
Gt. Ouse Chalk
Thames Chalk

River supply
River to river aqueducts
Bulk supply acqueducts

Rainfall in Britain is more than enough to meet our water needs. However, there is a problem!

If you have a go at Activity 5 you will be able to discuss what the problem is.

The problem of supply and demand is solved by moving water from areas that have plenty of water to areas that have little water. The first pipeline to do such a job was constructed in 1892 to transfer water from Wales to Birmingham. It is still being used today. But pipelines are very expensive and where possible natural river channels are used. For example, the River Severn is now used to transfer water from the reservoirs in Mid-Wales to the West Midlands. Figure 7 shows where the main reservoirs in England and Wales are located, and how water is moved from self-sufficient areas to areas of need.

WATER DISTRIBUTION

After leaving the Treatment Plant, the water is delivered to our towns through pipes known as WATER MAINS. They vary in size from 3 metres in diameter down to 25 mm diameter. The size depends on the population of the town it supplies. Today the pipes are made of plastic, but in the past they have been made of lead, iron, and copper.

WATER IN THE HOME
Diagram of water circulation in a typical house

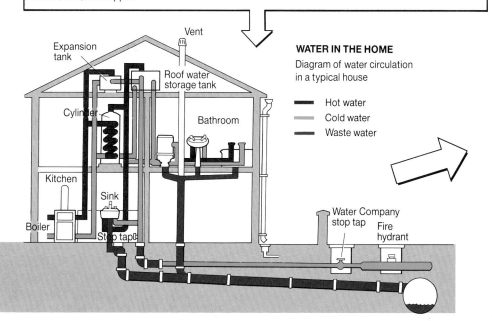

THE FINISHED PRODUCT
Clean drinking water

Activities

3 Look at Figure 6, which shows the human water cycle. In your own words, explain what each of these words mean:
Aquifer Filtration Water main Coagulation Borehole

4 Look at the 'water treatment' section of the diagram and explain why:
a) lime is added to the water, and
b) chlorine is added.

5 a) Using your atlas, find a map showing rainfall distribution in Britain. The rainfall map indicates which parts of the country have the greatest supply of water. Describe the distribution of rainfall in the country by firstly listing all the places with very high rainfall. Then list the areas with very low rainfall.

b) Now find a map showing where all the towns and cities in Britain are. This map shows you where the population is distributed, and therefore where the greatest demand for water is likely to be. Describe the distribution of population in the country.

c) Compare the two maps. Can you now say what the problem of Britain's water supply is?

6 Using the information in Figure 6, draw your own cartoon sequence showing the continuing story of Walter Droplet as he travels through the human water cycle.

7 Research idea:
Find out where your water comes from. Your local water authority will be able to give you all the details.

3 Our polluted waters

Figure 1 The effects of water pollution: dead fish in the Netherlands

The photograph shows what people can do with our water. We have in places turned clear, sparkling rivers, lakes, and seas into poisonous dumping grounds for our rubbish.

Figure 2 shows the major causes of water pollution. All living things, including humans, suffer because of the pollution.

Some chemicals, such as fertilisers, can cause particular problems. They greatly enrich the water so that there is a massive increase in the amount of tiny algae there. The water turns green, and a scum appears on the surface. The light is cut down, and plants begin to die, including the algae. Bacteria increases, and speeds up the decay so that the oxygen in the water is reduced. The water eventually becomes 'sealed off' from the air. The river and everything in it is dead.

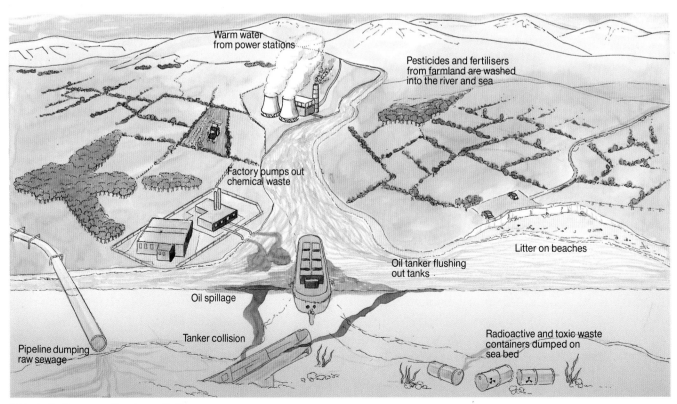

Figure 2 Sources of water pollution

NORTH SEA CHOKES TO DEATH ON ITS FILTH

The North Sea is the cesspit of Europe. It is polluted with litter, oil, algal blooms, toxic waste, radioactivity, and untreated sewage.

Parts of the rivers flowing into the sea have been declared biologically dead. The Scheldt, Europe's dirtiest river, supplies the sea with raw sewage from the 1.6 million people of Brussels. Scientists have shown that, in some areas of the North Sea, half the fish are severely deformed. The first warnings about the pollution in the North Sea came in 1967. An international team of scientists advised drastic action. But nothing happened! None of the eight countries that surround the sea saw it as their problem. Britain, known as 'the dirty man of Europe', believed that the dumping of waste did not cause any problems, and that the sea cleaned itself. Ideas have changed. In 1987, the eight countries met again and signed an agreement to reduce North Sea pollution by 50 per cent by 1995. Unfortunately, it appears unlikely they will achieve their aim. The poisoning of the North Sea seems set to continue.

Figure 3 A newspaper extract

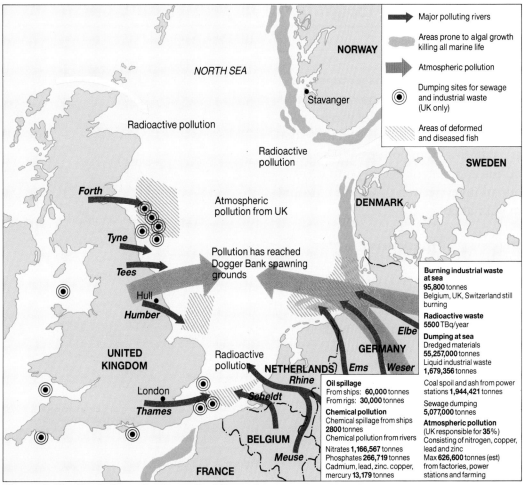

Figure 4 The North Sea – the 'cesspit of Europe'

Activities

1 Look at the photograph of water pollution in Figure 1. Describe what the picture shows and explain what might have caused the pollution.

2 Figure 2 shows the main causes of water pollution. Work in pairs to try to solve some of the pollution problems. Can you think of a way that three of the sources of pollution could be reduced?

3 Read the newspaper article on pollution in the North Sea carefully. Look also at the map (Figure 4).
a) List the eight countries that surround the North Sea.
b) The EC's Environment Commissioner has asked you to design a leaflet about pollution in the North Sea. The leaflet is going to be sent to all the industrial companies in the eight countries surrounding the North Sea. The aims of the leaflet are:
(i) to tell industries how bad the pollution problem is in the North Sea;
(ii) to tell industries what they can do to help solve the pollution problem.
The leaflet should be made of one piece of A4 paper, which can be folded in any way you like. It should be clear, attractive, and informative.

4 Assignment: Is your stream clean?

Background information

We have all seen newspaper reports or heard stories about the polluted rivers and streams in Britain. Do you know whether the water sources around you are suffering from pollution? The aim of this assignment is for you to carry out an investigation of water pollution in your area.

One way of measuring water quality

You can measure how clean stream and river water is without using any expensive equipment. The method involves looking at the kinds of animals that are found in the water.

Some animals need very clean water to live in. If the water is polluted in any way, then these animals will not survive. On the other hand, there are some animals that are able to live in polluted water. Figure 1 shows the animals that you may find in a stream or river.

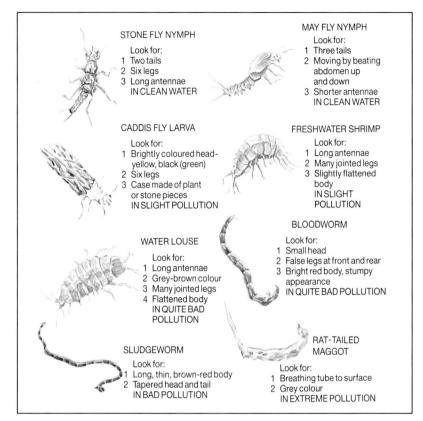

STONE FLY NYMPH
Look for:
1 Two tails
2 Six legs
3 Long antennae
IN CLEAN WATER

MAY FLY NYMPH
Look for:
1 Three tails
2 Moving by beating abdomen up and down
3 Shorter antennae
IN CLEAN WATER

CADDIS FLY LARVA
Look for:
1 Brightly coloured head-yellow, black (green)
2 Six legs
3 Case made of plant or stone pieces
IN SLIGHT POLLUTION

FRESHWATER SHRIMP
Look for:
1 Long antennae
2 Many jointed legs
3 Slightly flattened body
IN SLIGHT POLLUTION

WATER LOUSE
Look for:
1 Long antennae
2 Grey-brown colour
3 Many jointed legs
4 Flattened body
IN QUITE BAD POLLUTION

BLOODWORM
Look for:
1 Small head
2 False legs at front and rear
3 Bright red body, stumpy appearance
IN QUITE BAD POLLUTION

SLUDGEWORM
Look for:
1 Long, thin, brown-red body
2 Tapered head and tail
IN BAD POLLUTION

RAT-TAILED MAGGOT
Look for:
1 Breathing tube to surface
2 Grey colour
IN EXTREME POLLUTION

Figure 1 Indicators of water pollution

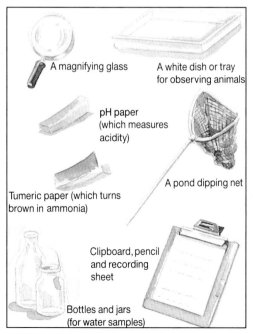

A magnifying glass

A white dish or tray for observing animals

pH paper (which measures acidity)

A pond dipping net

Tumeric paper (which turns brown in ammonia)

Clipboard, pencil and recording sheet

Bottles and jars (for water samples)

Figure 2 Equipment you will need in your investigation

Your assignment

Your assignment is to carry out a fieldwork investigation of water quality on one or more of your local streams and rivers. The way to carry out your investigations is outlined in the five steps below.

Step 1 – Choosing the site.
If possible, you want to *either*
a) compare pollution levels in two or more rivers or streams, *or*
b) measure how pollution levels change down the course of one river or stream.

Step 2 – Equipment.
The equipment you will need is illustrated in Figure 2.

Step 3 – Recording results.
You will need to prepare a recording sheet like the one in Figure 4.

WARNING
1. COLLECT SAMPLES WITH A FRIEND
2. BE CAREFUL OF DEEP AND FAST MOVING WATER
3. DON'T PADDLE BAREFOOT IN POLLUTED WATER
4. DON'T DRINK STREAM WATER

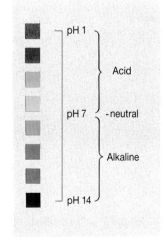

pH 1
Acid
pH 7 — neutral
Alkaline
pH 14

Figure 3 A pH chart

Step 4 – Taking measurements and making observations.

Read the warning sign carefully before you carry out these experiments.

You will need to repeat each test three times at each site, to make sure your results are not freak ones.

a) The pH test.
Fill your dish with stream water. Place a piece of indicator paper in the water. Read the pH by comparing it with the indicator chart (see Figure 3). Only marked differences in pH readings are significant.

b) The ammonia test.
Use the tumeric paper to test the water. If the paper turns brown then ammonia is present in the water. Ammonia is a deadly chemical that builds up in the water after the dumping of sewage, rotting vegetation, and carbon-based chemicals.

c) The minibeast survey.
Scoop your net through the weeds and over the stream bed. Clear excess mud out of the net by swishing it in running water. Empty the net into your dish and watch for the indicator minibeasts shown in Figure 1. You will need to use a magnifying glass or hand lens to be able to identify them properly. If you recognise any of them, tick them off on your record sheet.

Once you have finished with your minibeasts, return them to the stream.

d) Water observations.
Fill your jar with water. Look at the suspended sediment and smell the water. Record your observations on your record sheet.

e) Site observations.
Record general observations of the site, such as width and speed of stream and surrounding land use.

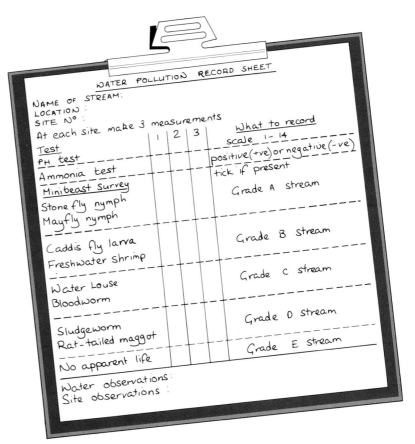

Figure 4 A water pollution record sheet

Step 5 – Writing up your results.

Write your report using the following sub-headings:

a) Introduction.
b) Fieldwork methods.
c) Results.
d) Explanation of results.
e) Conclusions.

Following up your investigation: taking action

If you have found there is a water pollution problem near you, perhaps you could do something about it. Working in small groups, plan a campaign to reduce water pollution in your area. Consider these ideas:
● Writing letters to the Council.
● An advertising campaign in school.
● Designing leaflets or posters for the general public, warning them of the dangers of water pollution and explaining how they can help solve the problem.

5 Too much water: Bangladesh

Abdul Korim. Paddy rice farmer in Bangladesh.

Just look at this - my wife and daughter marooned by the floods. We've lost everything - yet again. My house, my two oxen, my fields of rice are all under water. We were lucky that we heard the warnings and managed to put some sort of raft together. Many people from this area have drowned. We've seen the bodies in the water, along with the crocodiles! I don't know how many people have been affected by these floods, but just three months ago 30 million Bangladeshis, including my family, were made homeless by floods. What are we going to do now? If we don't drown or get eaten by the crocodiles we will probably starve to death, or catch cholera or typhoid from unclean water. There is no hope for us.

Figure 1 The plight of Abdul Korim, a paddy rice farmer in Bangladesh

Figure 2 Comparisons between Bangladesh and Britain

Abdul and his family survived the country's worst floods in December 1988. The flood water covered two-thirds of the country, caused 2300 deaths, and resulted in $1.3 billion of damage. Living in Bangladesh, one of the poorest countries of the world, the lives of farming families such as Abdul's have never been easy. Frequent flooding adds to the difficulties many families face.

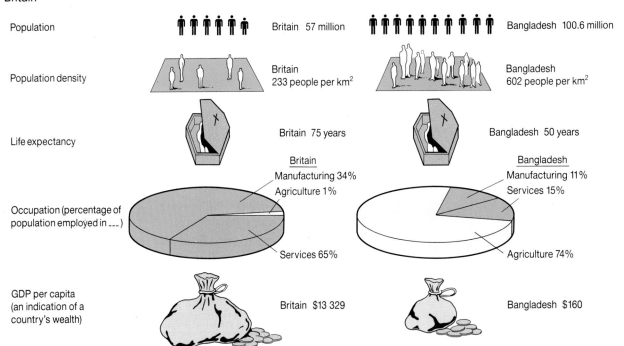

Population — Britain 57 million — Bangladesh 100.6 million

Population density — Britain 233 people per km² — Bangladesh 602 people per km²

Life expectancy — Britain 75 years — Bangladesh 50 years

Occupation (percentage of population employed in ___)

Britain
Manufacturing 34%
Agriculture 1%
Services 65%

Bangladesh
Manufacturing 11%
Services 15%
Agriculture 74%

GDP per capita (an indication of a country's wealth) — Britain $13 329 — Bangladesh $160

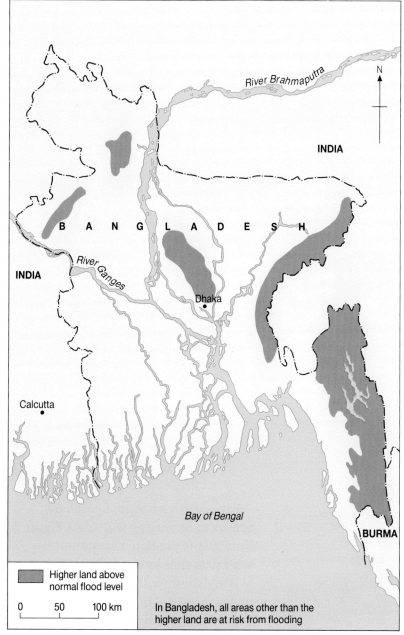

Figure 3 Bangladesh (look also at the world map on page 94)

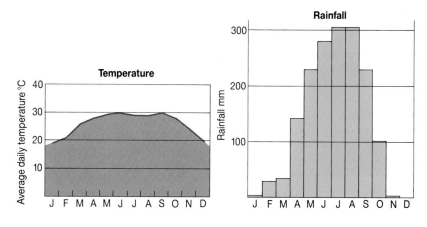

Between 1960 and 1981, Bangladesh was struck by 37 cyclones. Relief organisations estimate well over one million people died as a result. In 1987 and 1988 the country recorded the worst floods in its history.

A number of factors have led to bad flooding in Bangladesh:

1 Most of the country is low-lying, as Figure 3 shows. 'Tidal waves' can flood huge areas, including entire islands.

2 There are many rivers and canals which spread flood water across a wide area.

3 Flood waters come down-river from heavy rain in India and Nepal as well as up-river from tidal surges. The cutting down of trees (deforestation) in parts of the Himalayas has resulted in an increase of this storm water from the north.

4 Heavy seasonal rainfall, such as that occurring in 1988, can swell the rivers.

5 Bangladesh has one of the highest population densities – an average of over 600 people per square kilometre. The high population density means that many people are affected in a small area, and this also makes evacuation difficult.

6 Buildings cannot withstand severe storms or floods. Most houses are made from local materials such as bamboo and are built on wooden stilts to avoid normal flood water.

7 There are no coastal defences, because the country cannot afford

Figure 4 A climate graph for Dhaka. Not all flooding in Bangladesh is a disaster. The floods of the monsoon season (May to October) are vital to the rice farmers. If the monsoon is late or poor, millions of people go hungry

them, and they would be very difficult to construct.

8 There are no advanced warning systems, and communications, such as radio or telephones, are very poor. It is, therefore, very difficult to predict or prevent disaster.

Bangladesh lies in the path of typhoons or tropical cyclones. These intense storms, known as hurricanes in the Caribbean, are highly destructive.

Typhoons (usually in autumn) begin as upward currents of warm, moist air over the tropical oceans. As they move they develop into powerful swirling masses of air and clouds. As they move up the Bay of Bengal the force of the wind drives water northwards. As the Bay of Bengal gets narrower and the sea becomes shallower water builds up to a storm surge. Figure 5 shows what happens.

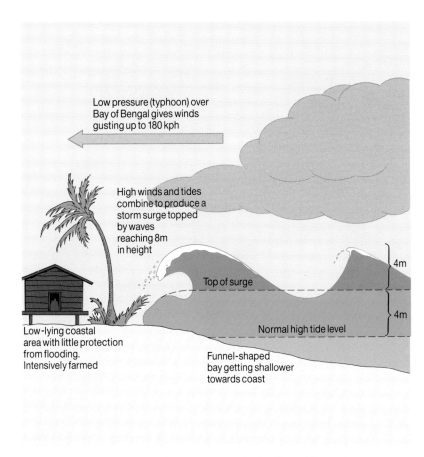

Figure 5 The development of a storm surge in the Bay of Bengal

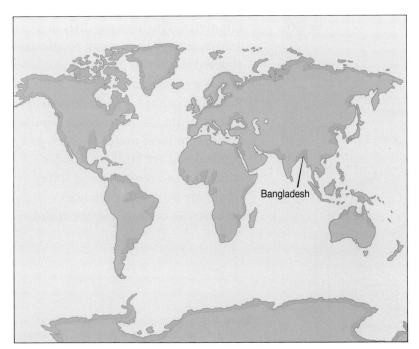

Figure 6 Will this be the shape of the world's coastlines by the year 2100? The dark blue areas show the parts of the world that could be drowned by a rise in sea-level

Bangladesh's flooding problems appear to be getting worse. As Figure 6 shows, it is predicted by some scientists that by the year 2100, most of Bangladesh will have disappeared under the sea. This rise in sea-level is expected if global temperature increases as a result of the 'greenhouse effect'. Scientists believe that the production of greenhouse gases, such as carbon dioxide, are causing temperatures to rise. Within 50 years, temperatures could rise by between 1.5 and 3.5°C. This global warming will melt the ice caps and glaciers, and alter world weather patterns. The sea-level could rise several metres. Low-lying countries such as Bangladesh could suffer the most.

Several solutions have been suggested for Bangladesh's flooding problem:

Scheme A: Build embankments along the whole of the Brahmaputra-Ganges-Meghna river system. The scheme should prevent serious flooding from the rivers, but not the coast. The embankments would take many years to build. Cost: $10 000 million.

Scheme B: Build dams and reservoirs in the upper waters of the rivers, to prevent flooding lower down. Dams would be built in India and Nepal, as well as Bangladesh. The reservoir water could be used for irrigation and generating electricity. The dams would not prevent flooding from tidal waves, or from heavy rainfall in central Bangladesh. Cost: $700 million.

Scheme C: Strengthen the banks of some of the rivers in Bangladesh, where the worst flooding occurs. Improve the flood warning system in the country. Improve irrigation schemes, with better drainage, in areas likely to flood. The scheme would not necessarily prevent flooding, but it would reduce its impact. Cost: $500 million.

Figure 7
The flooded streets of Dhaka

Activities

1 Using the data in Figure 2, make a comparison between Britain and Bangladesh.

2 Study the climate graph for Dhaka.
  a) Which is the wettest month?
  b) What is the temperature in July?
  c) What is the annual range in temperature (the difference between the warmest and the coldest months)?

3 Imagine you lived near to the coast in Bangladesh. A tropical cyclone is heading for the coast. Write a diary about your experience as the cyclone reaches your village.

4 In recent years Bangladesh has suffered from frequent serious flooding. In your own words, explain how each of these factors is linked to the flood problem facing Bangladesh:
  a) The climate of the region.
  b) The relief of the country.
  c) The number of people living in Bangladesh.
  d) The fact that Bangladesh is a poor country.

5 If the scientists prove to be right about the greenhouse effect, the future of Bangladesh, and some other low-lying parts of the world, looks bleak. What could be done to reduce the threat of floods?

6 a) For each of the flood-protection schemes mentioned on this page, list the main advantages and disadvantages.
  b) Which of the schemes would you choose? Explain why.
  c) Can you think of a better way of dealing with the flood hazard? Describe your own scheme.

6 Too little water: the Sahel

Yemani Gebre. Umballa refugee camp, Sudan.

We've been here for weeks now - waiting to see who will be the next to die. It was three years ago that the first rains failed. Our crops all dried up and my father had to sell six of our thirty cattle to buy food. The following year was even worse. Soldiers took all of our grain and some of our cattle, and the rains failed again. The village water hole dried up and my mother had to walk twelve miles to find water. My father decided to sell the rest of our cattle. We spent all our money on six months supply of grain. My sister became ill with tuberculosis, and we did not have any money to buy medicines, so she died. When our grain ran out we begged from friends and relatives in the village. Our last hope was to make it to a refugee camp. It took us two weeks to get here.

Figure 1 The plight of Yemani Gebre, a Sudanese refugee

The Sudan is a country which lies at the eastern end of the Sahel. 'Sahel' is the Arab word for 'fringe' or 'shore' and is used to describe the southern end of the Sahara Desert. Figure 3 shows that the Sahel usually has a wet season during the summer months, but that virtually no rain falls for the rest of the year. Since 1968, there have been several very dry years. As a result, crops could not grow and famine set in. Between 1968 and 1973 it is estimated that 250 000 people and 3.5 million animals died in the Sahel as a result of drought. In recent years the figures have been even higher.

One effect of the lack of rainfall is the gradual spreading of the Sahara. This is known as desertification. The southern edge of the Sahara is expanding at an average of 10 km per year.

The actions of people have made the situation worse. The rapid population growth in parts of the Sahel has increased the pressure on the already fragile environment. Trees are felled for firewood and housebuilding, thus removing protection for the soil from

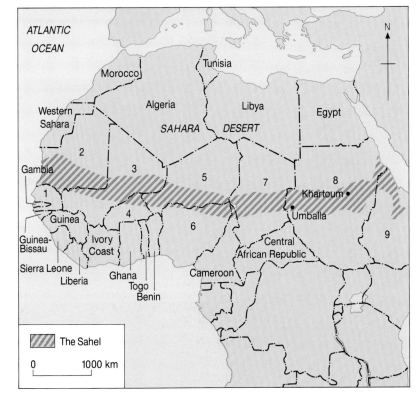

Figure 2 The Sahel

	J	F	M	A	M	J	J	A	S	O	N	D
Average daily temperature (°C)	23	24	27	28	29	29	27	26	27	28	26	24
Average monthly rainfall (mm)	3	3	3	3	3	7	55	75	15	5	4	0

Figure 3 Climate data for Khartoum, the capital of Sudan

strong winds and heavy rain. Grazing too many animals in one area (overgrazing) and the continuous growing of crops in the same field also result in the soil rapidly becoming infertile.

The short-term solution to drought and famine is for aid organisations, such as Oxfam and Save the Children Fund, to send food and medical supplies to areas of need. However important this may be at the time, it is not a long-term solution.

The problem is the water supply. Water needs to be stored in the wet season for use in the long dry season. There are many water projects in the Sahel. Some are large-scale, costing a great deal of money, while others are small-scale and cheap to run.

Large-scale projects involve the construction of dams and reservoirs, with irrigation channels leading from the reservoir to the crops. One project, costing $1 billion, supplies areas of Senegal, Mali, and Mauritania with a constant supply of water for farming, drinking, and electricity production.

Small-scale schemes are usually fairly cheap to install. They involve the drilling of deep water wells, the installation of water pumps, and the building of simple irrigation channels. For small villages these are the ideal solutions. Some countries have also begun to realise how important trees are in preventing the spread of the desert. In Mauritania, volunteers go into the desert daily to plant and water young trees.

Large quantities of grain are lost each year because of poor storage facilities. If the grain gets wet it will rot, and if pests can get to the grain they will eat large quantities of it. Much has been done to try and improve storage facilities by building stores like the maize crib in Figure 4.

Figure 4 A maize crib

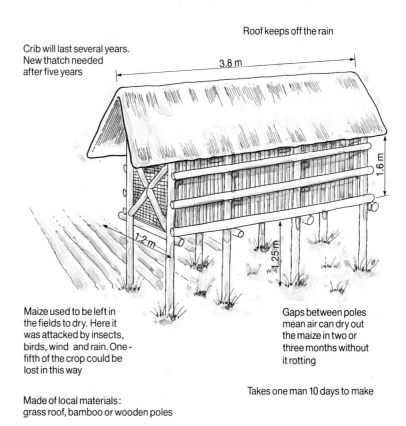

Crib is like a well-ventilated box

Roof keeps off the rain

Crib will last several years. New thatch needed after five years

3.8 m

1.6 m

1.25 m

1.2 m

Maize used to be left in the fields to dry. Here it was attacked by insects, birds, wind and rain. One-fifth of the crop could be lost in this way

Gaps between poles mean air can dry out the maize in two or three months without it rotting

Takes one man 10 days to make

Made of local materials: grass roof, bamboo or wooden poles

Activities

1 Using Figure 2 as a guide, draw your own map of the Sahel. Use the world map on page 94 to name the countries numbered 1–9 on your map.

2 Use the climate data in Figure 3 to draw climate graphs for Khartoum.

3 Why do you think food aid is not a long-term solution for Yemani Gebre and his family?

4 When Yemani Gebre and his family return to their village, do you think they would benefit more from one large-scale project or several small-scale schemes?

5 In your own words, explain how people who live in the Sahel have helped to cause desertification.

1 Introducing Italy

You probably have in your mind some images of what Italy is like – even if you have never been there. What are your images of Italy? Where did your images of Italy come from?

Figure 1 compares Italy and the United Kingdom. The information shows that in some ways the two countries are similar – their population size is almost the same, for example. Yet in other ways they are very different. Most of Italy is very much a Mediterranean country. The narrow 'boot' shape of Italy means that nowhere is very far from the Mediterranean Sea. Apart from the mainland, Italy also has two large islands, Sicily and Sardinia. In this unit you will be looking at Italy as a country, and finding out something about its physical landscape and about its people and industries.

Data File Italy and the UK compared		
	ITALY	**UK**
Area	301 300 km^2	244 046 km^2
Population	57 million	56 million
Population density	196 per km^2	237 per km^2
Language	Italian	English
Religion	Mainly Roman Catholic	Mainly Protestant
Currency	Lire	Pounds
Capital	Rome	London
	Member of the EC	Member of the EC
	Mainland and islands in Mediterranean Sea in southern Europe. About 75% hills and mountains. Most flat land in north.	Group of large and small islands in Atlantic Ocean off north-west Europe. Hills and mountains in north-west, most flat land in south and east.

Figure 1

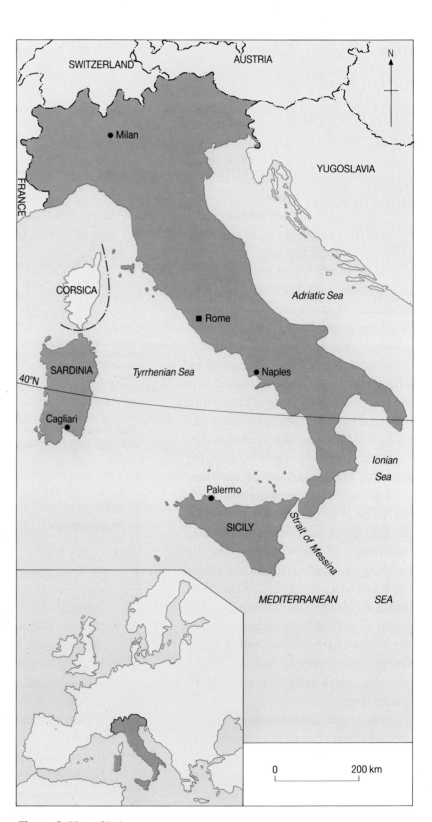

Figure 2 Map of Italy

Figure 3 This map shows the twenty districts of Italy and the eight districts of the Mezzogiorno

Italy is divided into twenty districts, as shown in Figure 3. In terms of way of life, the most obvious divide is between the north and south of the country. The South is often called the Mezzogiorno. Mezzogiorno, in Italian, means 'midday'. The name comes from the heat of the midday sun that beats down on southern Italy in the summer. Today, the average standard of living in the South is lower than in the North. In the past the standard of living gap was even wider – Figure 4 compares North and South in 1950. Even though the government has tried to close the wealth gap, there is still a distinct North-South Divide in Italy.

Activities

1 Using Figure 2, and your atlas if you need to, draw your own map of Italy, which shows:
   a) the two largest Italian islands;
   b) the seas surrounding Italy;
   c) the other countries bordering Italy;
   d) the capital city and other larger cities.
2 Write a paragraph to describe the location of Italy in Europe – you could use lines of longitude and latitude.
3 Compare Italy with the United Kingdom. Using the Data File in Figure 1 and your own knowledge, make two lists showing *similarities* and *differences*.
4 Where and what is the Mezzogiorno? Show the Mezzogiorno on your map of Italy.
5 What is meant by the North-South Divide in Italy? What does the information in Figure 4 tell us about the differences in the standard of living for people in Italy in 1950.

ITEM	SOUTH	NORTH
Total land area (%)	40	60
Total population (%)	38	62
Percentage employed in:		
a Agriculture	53	37
b Industry & transport	27	39
c Commerce	20	24
Consumption of electricity (kWh per head)	141	612
Cars and motorcycles per 1000 inhabitants	53	156
Average food consumption (kg/per head)	16	37
Percentage of population below the 'poverty line'	27	3

Figure 4 Comparing the South and the North of Italy, 1950

2 The physical environment

When studying a country one of the important things to look at is its physical environment. By this we mean what the natural landscape and climate are like. Is it mountainous or flat? Is it hot or cold, wet or dry? Is the land fertile or barren? In Italy there are many contrasts in physical environment. It is one of the differences between the North and South.

As Figure 1 shows, much of Italy is hilly or mountainous. In the very north, where Italy joins the rest of the continent of Europe, lie the Alps, the highest mountains in Europe. 'Peninsular' Italy is dominated by the Apennine Mountains, which form a spine of highland running down the country. The islands too are largely mountainous. The only large area of flatter land is the Lombardy Plain, in the north.

In terms of climate, all of Italy has very warm summers and mild winters. Only in the mountains do winter temperatures fall below freezing. The summer climate becomes hotter and drier as you move south. The graphs show the climate in Rome, roughly in the centre of the country. Here, and further north, there is some rain in every month. Moving south of Rome, into the Mezzogiorno, the summers are very hot and dry.

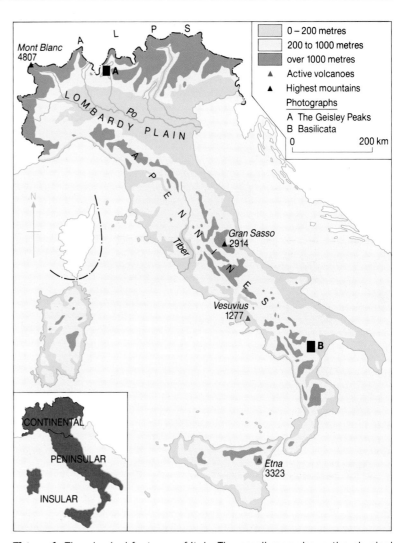

Figure 1 The physical features of Italy. The small map shows the physical divides

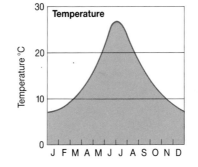
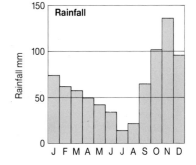

Figure 2 Climate graphs for Rome

	J	F	M	A	M	J	J	A	S	O	N	D
Average monthly temperature (°C)	11	12	13	15	18	22	25	26	23	20	17	13
Average monthly rainfall (mm)	70	40	50	50	20	10	0	20	40	75	65	55

Figure 3 Climate data for Palermo, Sicily

Figure 4 The Geisley Peaks and Southern Magdalena in the Dolomites, northern Italy (see Figure 1)

Figure 5 Peasant agriculture in Basilicata, southern Italy (see Figure 1)

Activities

1 Using Figure 1, and your atlas if you need to, draw your own map of Italy's physical features.
   a) Shade in the land over 200 metres.
   b) Mark and name some high mountains and volcanoes.
   c) Mark and name the two longest rivers.
   d) Name the largest area of flatter land.
   Remember to give your map a title and key.

2 a) Write a paragraph to describe the climate in Rome. Write first about the temperatures over the year, then about the pattern of rainfall.
   b) Use the data in Figure 3 to construct your own climate graphs for Palermo.
   c) What are the main differences between the climates of Rome and Palermo?

3 Look at the two photographs of country areas – their locations are marked A and B on Figure 1. What evidence is there in each photo about:
   a) the time of the year;
   b) the climate of the area;
   c) the way people earn their living;
   d) the standard of living for local people.

4 The small map in Figure 1 divides Italy into three physical regions. In your own words, explain the meaning of the three words used.

3 People and history

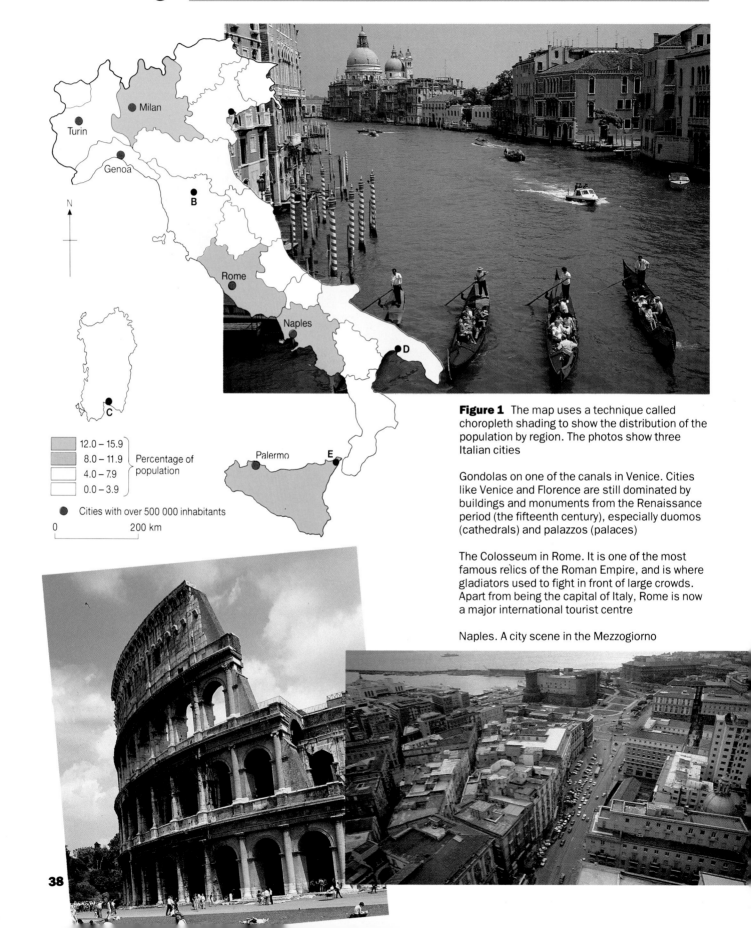

Figure 1 The map uses a technique called choropleth shading to show the distribution of the population by region. The photos show three Italian cities

Gondolas on one of the canals in Venice. Cities like Venice and Florence are still dominated by buildings and monuments from the Renaissance period (the fifteenth century), especially duomos (cathedrals) and palazzos (palaces)

The Colosseum in Rome. It is one of the most famous relics of the Roman Empire, and is where gladiators used to fight in front of large crowds. Apart from being the capital of Italy, Rome is now a major international tourist centre

Naples. A city scene in the Mezzogiorno

Percentage of population

12.0 – 15.9
8.0 – 11.9
4.0 – 7.9
0.0 – 3.9

● Cities with over 500 000 inhabitants

0   200 km

Living in Britain is different from living in, say, India, or the USA, or Hong Kong, or Jamaica. All countries are different in some ways, as they have their own character.

What is it that makes Italy different? It sounds a simple question, but in fact it is a very hard one to answer. You could say the obvious things – like the language, or the money, or some of the food and drink. Yet the question 'what makes Italy different' goes much deeper than that. Every country has had a different history. Italy's history has been long and varied. Figure 2 tells you a little about the times and people who have had an influence on Italian history and its people today.

Italy's people are not spread evenly, as the map in Figure 1 shows. It highlights the four regions where there are concentrations of population. The large majority of Italians live in towns and cities, most in smaller towns of about 20 000 people or less. No single city dominates Italy in the way that London is very much the most important city in Britain, or in the way Paris dominates France.

The cities of Italy are another way of looking at North-South differences. Early in their histories the big cities of the North, such as Milan, Turin, Genoa, and Venice, became major centres for trade and making goods. The great wealth created by their trade allowed the cities to become important places for culture and the arts – for architecture, painting, writing, and sculpture. One high point of Italian culture came in the period called the Renaissance in the fifteenth century. Today, the towns and cities of the North are still Italy's most important industrial centres.

In the South the larger cities, such as Naples and Palermo, never grew as major trading or industrial centres. The standard of living is lower than in the wealthier northern cities. In some ways Mezzogiorno cities have things in common with cities in the less developed countries of the world. In Naples many thousands of people live in slum dwellings. The city, of almost a million people, did not have a public sewerage system until the mid-1970s.

Figure 2 A brief history of Italy

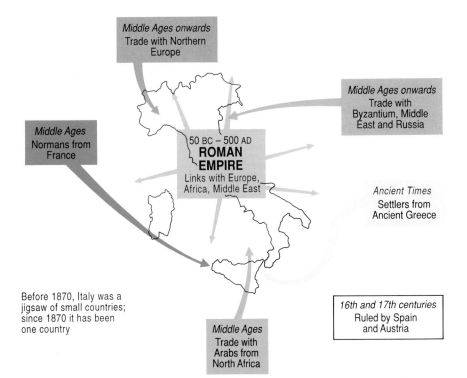

Middle Ages onwards
Trade with Northern Europe

Middle Ages onwards
Trade with Byzantium, Middle East and Russia

Middle Ages
Normans from France

50 BC – 500 AD
ROMAN EMPIRE
Links with Europe, Africa, Middle East

Ancient Times
Settlers from Ancient Greece

Before 1870, Italy was a jigsaw of small countries; since 1870 it has been one country

Middle Ages
Trade with Arabs from North Africa

16th and 17th centuries
Ruled by Spain and Austria

Figure 3

ITALY - Population Fact File	
Total population	57 million
Population density	196 per km²
Largest city	Rome, 2.8 m
Cities of over 500 000	6
Urban population	69%
Rural population	31%

Activities

1 a) On a map of Italy, mark and name the six largest cities.
   b) Use your atlas to mark and name on your map the cities labelled A–E on Figure 1.
2 Using Figure 1, describe the distribution of population across the regions of Italy.
3 A difficult question . . .
   Thinking about Britain (or another country you know very well), what do *you* feel are the things which make the country different from others?
   Think of a good way of showing your ideas – either in writing or as diagrams.

4 Economic contrasts

The North-South Divide in Italy can be seen in the way people earn their living – in farming and industry.

In all regions of the South, the Mezzogiorno, the number of people who depend on farming for their living is much higher than the national average. Yet in many parts of the Mezzogiorno the land provides only a poor living – what is called peasant farming. Almost half the area is mountainous. Summer drought is a problem except where irrigation is possible. Farming is an important activity, but farms are usually very small. These small farms are known as minifundia. They are typically less than three hectares in size, and they are divided into a number of scattered small plots, which are used to grow wheat, olives, or fruit, or to raise livestock. The majority of farming families do not own their own land. The most productive farmland in Italy is in the North, in the basin of the River Po. Here the soils are fertile, and water is more readily available for irrigating crops.

Over the past thirty years Italy has become one of the most important industrial countries in Europe. There has been a growth of industry in all parts of the country. Even so, there continues to be a far greater concentration of industry in the North, particularly in what is known as the Industrial Triangle. Why is this? Traditionally, industry has flourished in the North. Today, northern Italy is closer to the rest of Europe – the markets where Italian firms need to sell their goods. The Mezzogiorno is isolated from the rest of Europe by distance, and by poor road and rail links.

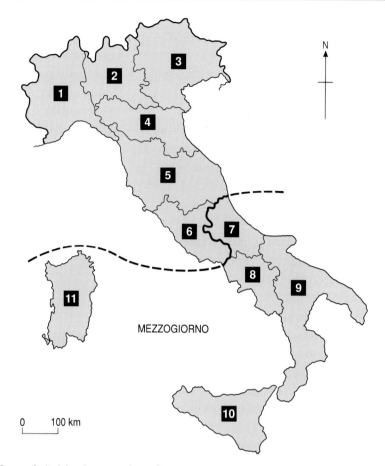

Figure 1 Italy's eleven main regions

Figure 2

Region	EMPLOYMENT INFORMATION	
	Number of workers employed in FARMING compared to the average for the whole of Italy	Number of workers employed in MANUFACTURING INDUSTRY compared to the average for the whole of Italy
1	Below Average	Above Average
2	Below Average	Above Average
3	Average	Average
4	Average	Average
5	Average	Average
6	Below Average	Below Average
7	Above Average	Below Average
8	Above Average	Below Average
9	Above Average	Below Average
10	Above Average	Below Average
11	Above Average	Below Average

The INDUSTRIAL TRIANGLE

The greatest concentration of Italian industry is in the area between the cities of Turin, Milan, and the port of Genoa. Turin is home to much of Italy's car industry. The region of Lombardy, including Milan, has 15 per cent of the country's people, but provides 40 per cent of Italy's exports from small and medium-sized firms.

Figure 3

Figure 4 The Fiat car works at Turin. Turin is part of the North's 'Industrial Triangle'

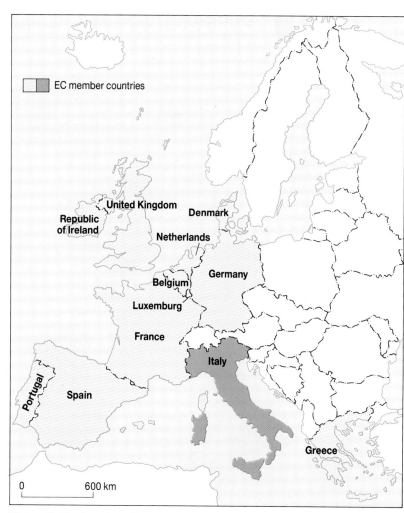

Figure 5 The location of Italy within the EC

Activities

1 a) What are minifundia?
b) Give some reasons why farming in the South is not very productive.

2 Most Mezzogiorno farms are small and worked by people who do not own the land. Why is this a disadvantage when it comes to trying to bring in more modern methods of farming?

3 Work in a pair.
a) Make two copies of the regions map in Figure 1.
b) Use the maps to show the information provided in Figure 2 by colour shading the regions.
c) Write down what your maps tell you about the way people earn their living in different parts of Italy.

4 What is Italy's Industrial Triangle? Draw a sketch map (by eye only, do not trace it) to show the location of the Industrial Triangle.

5 Unemployment and emigration

Emigration is the process by which people move voluntarily from one area to another.

A person is said to be *unemployed* when he/she does not have a job of any kind.

Figure 1 The map shows the per capita income for each region in 1950. The table shows the percentage share of unemployment by region for 1984

The contrast in wealth between the North and South of Italy has affected the people of the Mezzogiorno in two main ways.

Firstly, the amount of unemployment in the regions of the South was very high. Jobs had not been created by industrial growth and with a growing population many people failed to find work. Even for those people who gained employment in agriculture and tourism, wages were still very low compared with the industrial areas of the North.

The second major impact of the North-South Divide has been emigration. Although over a third of Italy's population still live in the Mezzogiorno, there has been a history of movement of people from the South towards the more prosperous regions of the North.

Figure 3 summarises the four main reasons for emigration from the South. Many people in the South earn their living from farming. The Mediterranean climate is very hot and dry for part of the year, and this has not helped developments in farming. Soils are generally poor and much of the land is hilly.

Many of the people who work in farming do not own their own land. Many workers are employed on huge estates called 'latifundia' and are paid low wages. For them, the attraction of jobs out of farming is high. But in the South there is much less industry to provide an alternative to jobs in farming. It is in the North that modern industry has expanded rapidly during this century.

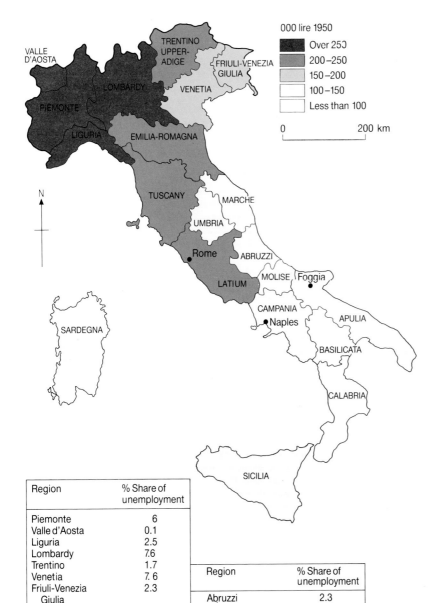

000 lire 1950

■	Over 250
▨	200–250
▨	150–200
□	100–150
□	Less than 100

0   200 km

Region	% Share of unemployment
Piemonte	6
Valle d'Aosta	0.1
Liguria	2.5
Lombardy	7.6
Trentino	1.7
Venetia	7.6
Friuli-Venezia Giulia	2.3
Emilia-Romagna	6.9
Tuscany	6.3
Umbria	1.6
Marche	2.6
Latium	8.8
Campania	9.6

Region	% Share of unemployment
Abruzzi	2.3
Molise	0.8
Apulia	6.9
Basilicata	1.1
Calabria	3.7
Sicilia	8.6
Sardegna	2.8

Region	Net emigration (1000s/annum)	
	1966	1985
Campania	26.4	1.7
Abruzzi/Molise	15.0	7.4
Apulia	27.5	0.3
Basilicata	8.6	-0.2
Calabria	23.3	4.6
Sicily	33.5	16.1
Sardinia	6.5	4.5
Total	140.8	34.4

Figure 2 Net emigration from the Mezzogiorno, 1966 and 1985

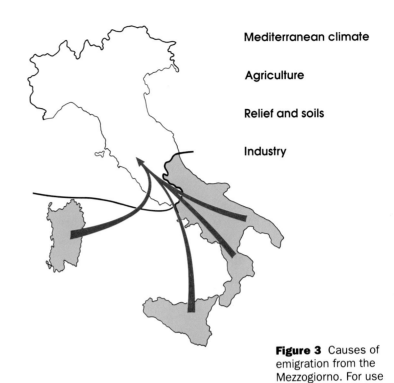

Mediterranean climate

Agriculture

Relief and soils

Industry

Figure 3 Causes of emigration from the Mezzogiorno. For use with Activity 4

Many of the migrants moving out of the South have been young people who have gone to look for jobs in the North or even other countries in Europe. This has also meant that the communities of the South have stagnated as only the very young and old remain to continue the way of life there. Often the migrants send back part of their earnings, but this is still not enough to increase the prosperity of the region. Those migrants who moved abroad travelled mainly to Europe, especially Switzerland, and North and South America (Brazil, Argentina, and Venezuela).

Figure 2 shows that in recent years emigration from the Mezzogiorno has slowed down. One reason for this is that there have been developments which have created more jobs in the South. People have even moved in to the Mezzogiorno. Some have come, for example, from countries in North Africa, where people are poorer still.

Activities

1 Name two regions of Italy which had per capita incomes of less than 100 000 lire per year in 1950.
2 Explain why the four regions of North-West Italy had the highest per capita incomes.
3 a) Construct your own choropleth map to show the distribution of unemployment by region, using the data in the table in Figure 1.
   b) What do you notice?
4 Make a neat copy of Figure 3. Using each heading, explain in your own words why this has been a cause of emigration from the South to the North.
5 Compile a map to show the destination of emigrants leaving the Mezzogiorno (this should include both locations within and outside Italy).
6 Describe how the pattern of emigration from the Mezzogiorno has changed between 1966 and 1985.

6 Finding a solution to the divide

In 1945, at the end of the Second World War and the fighting which raged over the Mezzogiorno, there was real poverty and hunger in southern Italy. Unemployment was widespread. It was time for the government at last to try to tackle the problem.

In 1950, the government set up a plan called the Cassa per il Mezzogiorno (The Southern Italy Fund). It was a bold move to channel money and new jobs into the South. The fund drew money from several sources, as Figure 5 on page 46 shows. Figure 3 summarises what the fund set out to achieve. Most people worked on the land, and so the concentration at first was on farming.

Improvements were also made to communications and services. These improvements were needed before industry – and jobs – could be attracted. New industry has been brought into the Mezzogiorno by offering companies incentives, such as lower taxes and not having to pay customs duties on imported raw materials. As Figure 2 shows, most of the new developments were heavy industries, such as steel making, oil refining, and petrochemicals. Industry was concentrated mainly in larger cities such as Naples, Brindisi, and Taranto.

Figure 1 'Success stories' in farming

> **In Apulia-Basilicata ...**
>
> Large farms, called latifundia, were owned by people who lived elsewhere. About 200 000 hectares of land was taken from absentee landowners, and given to 31 000 poor farming families. Production improved.

> **In Campania ...**
>
> In more fertile farming areas owners of small farms joined together to form co-operatives to market their fruit and vegetables, which were being produced more efficiently.

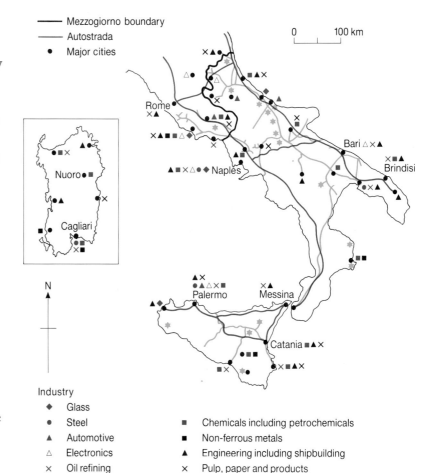

Industry
- ◆ Glass
- ● Steel
- ▲ Automotive
- △ Electronics
- × Oil refining
- — Pipelines

- ■ Chemicals including petrochemicals
- ■ Non-ferrous metals
- ▲ Engineering including shipbuilding
- × Pulp, paper and products
- ✳ Natural gas production

Figure 2 The map shows developments in roads and industry in the Mezzogiorno. The photo shows the inside of a steel plant near Naples

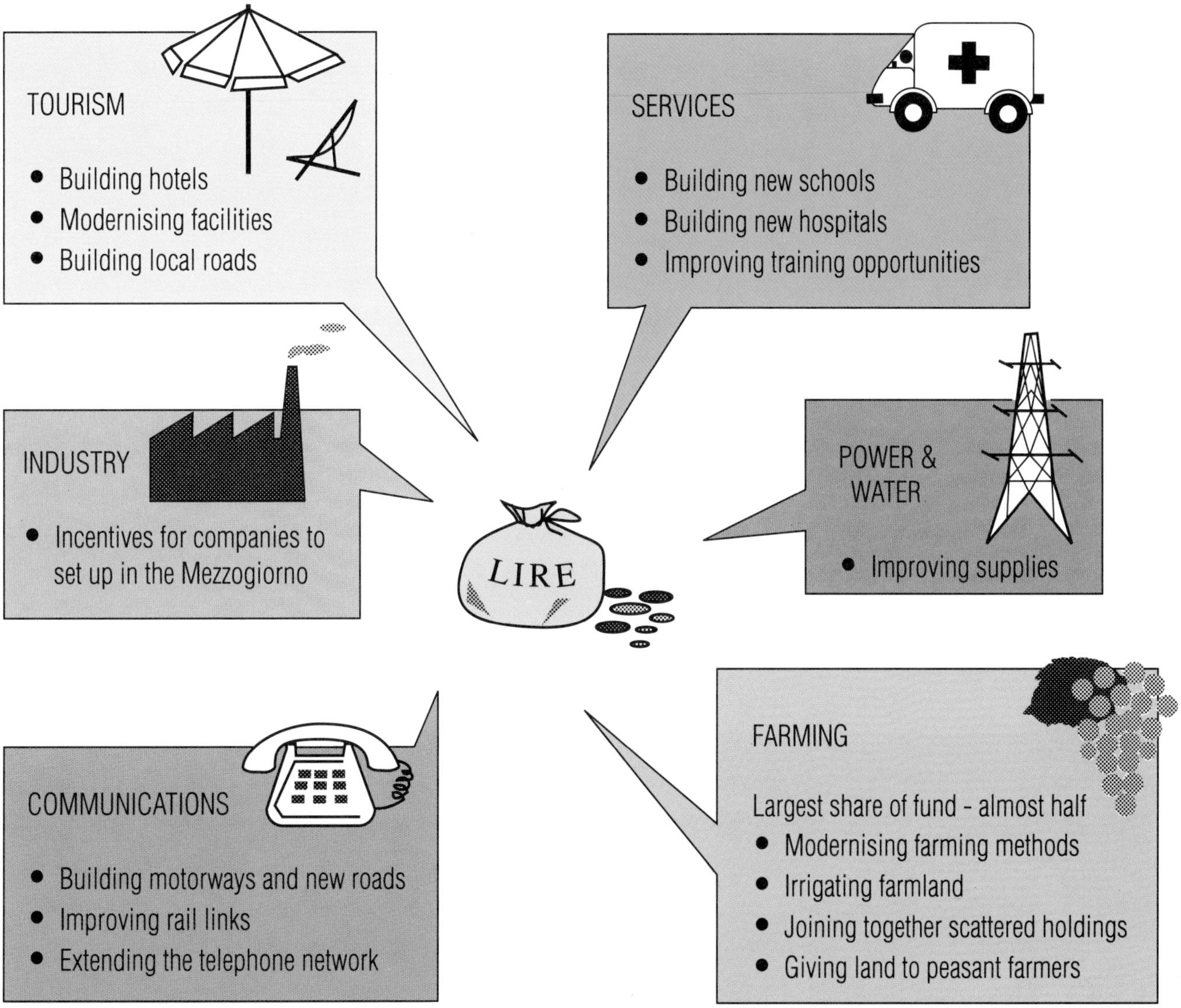

TOURISM

- Building hotels
- Modernising facilities
- Building local roads

SERVICES

- Building new schools
- Building new hospitals
- Improving training opportunities

INDUSTRY

- Incentives for companies to set up in the Mezzogiorno

LIRE

POWER & WATER

- Improving supplies

COMMUNICATIONS

- Building motorways and new roads
- Improving rail links
- Extending the telephone network

FARMING

Largest share of fund - almost half
- Modernising farming methods
- Irrigating farmland
- Joining together scattered holdings
- Giving land to peasant farmers

Figure 3 What the Cassa has spent its money on

Figure 4 A tourist development in Sardinia

45

Figure 5 Sources of funding for the Cassa per il Mezzogiorno

	NORTH		SOUTH		SOUTH AS A % OF NORTH	
	1951	1971	1951	1971	1951	1971
Industrial workforce (thousands)	3508	5540	734	984	38.8	33.1
Income per capita (000 lire at current prices)	193	1267	104	684	53.8	54.0
Number of telephones per 100 inhabitants	4.2	21.1	0.8	10.3	19.0	48.8
Number of cars per 100 inhabitants	1.9	24.2	0.7	13.9	36.8	57.4
Number of hospital beds per 1000 inhabitants	9.2	11.9	4.3	8.0	46.7	67.2

Figure 6 Comparing the South and the North to show the effects of the Cassa per il Mezzogiorno

Figure 7 The autostrada below Taormina, Sicily: one of the new roads in the South

Unfortunately, the number of jobs created elsewhere has not been as many as had been hoped for.

Has the Cassa per il Mezzogiorno been a success? Yes and no is the answer. There have been some good results. For example, emigration has slowed down, and some people have even been returning. Jobs have been created to allow some people to leave the poverty of peasant farming. Employment in agriculture has fallen from 57 per cent in 1950 to 19 per cent in 1986. The benefits have been patchy though, and people in some poorer areas have hardly been affected by the changes.

What about the wealth gap between the North and South? Figure 6 shows some changes that came about in the first twenty years of the fund. There has been a very real improvement in the standard of living for people in the Mezzogiorno. Unfortunately, the wealth gap has not closed. Average incomes in the South are still almost half those in the North. The government recognises that it will have to continue to fund change in the Mezzogiorno. Developing tourism is one approach.

Perhaps a different way of bringing jobs and money to the South might be what is called the 'Third Italy' idea. This refers to the small firms and workshops which are emerging in the central regions from Umbria to Veneto and Fruili-Venezia Giulia. Large northern companies have invested a lot of money in these small, specialised firms. For example, seven villages in Southern Marche produce 25 per cent of Italy's shoes, and the Benettons are world-famous entrepreneurs of the Third Italy. This region also possesses mixed farming and rural crafts, and tourist resorts and fishing ports along the coast.

Figure 8 Small businesses are characteristic of the Third Italy. This photo shows a workshop in Naples making soft toys

Activities

1 What was the Cassa per il Mezzogiorno? Explain in your own words:
   a) where it was set up;
   b) why it was set up;
   c) who started it;
   d) where the money came from.
2 Draw your own diagram to show what the Cassa per il Mezzogiorno set out to achieve.
3 How successful do you think the Cassa per il Mezzogiorno has been? Use the ideas in the text and the information in Figure 6 in your answer.
4 Work in a pair or small group. You are a planning team, working for the Italian government. What ideas do you have for trying to close the wealth gap between North and South Italy? Think of a good way of presenting your ideas to the rest of the class.

7 Assignment: Hazards and tourism

> A *natural hazard* is an extreme natural process or event which may put people's lives in danger.

Your assignment

The purpose of this assignment is for you to explore whether the Mezzogiorno can develop its tourist industry. Many tourists already visit the South, but there is scope for tourism to grow further. This will bring more money into the region's economy and so aid its development. In particular, you should see whether the different natural hazards which occur in the South can be used as an advantage to attract tourists to the area.

A land of disasters

Italy experiences a wide range of natural hazards. Seventy per cent of the country is at risk from earthquakes, landslides, floods, and avalanches. These have caused over 135 000 deaths since the start of the century.

Earthquakes (violent shakings of the ground set off by movements in the earth's crust) are the greatest hazard because 32 per cent of the population live in high risk areas. Figure 1 shows that a large number of the more severe earthquakes also occur in the Mezzogiorno. For example, in 1908 the city of Messina on Sicily was devastated by an earthquake that caused a series of damaging tidal waves.

Many areas in the South are also at risk from landslides. These are often triggered by an earthquake event, such as that in 1980 which caused landslides in thirty-six settlements, but are also due to farming practices. Where hill pastures have been overgrazed by sheep and goats serious soil erosion is often the consequence.

Italy also boasts two of the world's most active volcanoes, both of which are located within the Mezzogiorno. Mount Vesuvius is situated 16 km east of Naples. It is famous for its eruption in AD 79. This buried the city of Herculaneum under a sea of boiling mud and smothered the city of Pompeii, 24 km away, under three to five metres of volcanic ash. Thousands of people were killed. Today many millions of people visit the site of Pompeii which has been completely excavated and is undergoing a lot of restoration work to preserve it for the

Figure 1 Map showing natural hazards in Italy

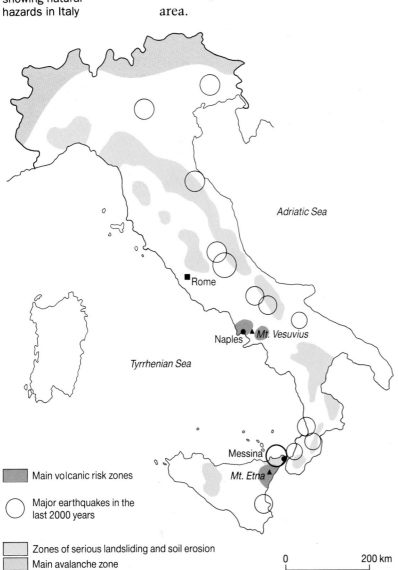

Adriatic Sea

Rome

Tyrrhenian Sea

Naples ▲ *Mt. Vesuvius*

Messina

Mt. Etna ▲

Main volcanic risk zones

◯ Major earthquakes in the last 2000 years

Zones of serious landsliding and soil erosion

Main avalanche zone

0   200 km

future. It is also possible to take a bus from Naples up the sides of the volcano and then walk the last few hundred metres to look into the crater. There have been a number of eruptions since AD 79, the most destructive being in 1631. A minor eruption took place in 1944.

Mount Etna, the largest active volcano in Europe, is located on the island of Sicily. It is 3323 metres high and is snow-capped for most of the year above 1800 metres. Despite the threat posed by Etna on the surrounding area, including the cities of Catania and Messina, this otherwise barren upper part of the volcano has already been partially developed as a winter sports centre.

Figure 2 A Sicilian village wrecked by an earthquake

Figure 3 A lava flow from Mount Etna engulfs a vineyard as insurance assessors look on

Figure 4 Mount Vesuvius is an important tourist attraction. This photo shows a group of tourists on the rim of the crater. Public access to the crater has been improved, and souvenir stalls sell items such as rocks and minerals from the crater and photographs of the surrounding countryside

Figure 5 This satellite image shows part of Sicily and the toe of the 'boot' of Italy. Mount Etna is clearly visible on the eastern side of the island. It is possible to identify the snow-capped peak, recent lava flows, and vegetation on the lower slopes

Figure 6 The Amphitheatre, Pompeii. This ancient Roman amphitheatre is one of the most prominent features of Pompeii. Unfortunately, it is now becoming overgrown with vegetation

Figure 7 Mount Etna. This photo was taken during the eruption of 1971

Mount Etna dominates to such an extent the eastern half of the island and has had such a terrible influence on the lives of so many from time immemorial that it is not surprising that in classical times it was the subject of legends, and has for long been the object of awe, fear, and superstition.

By the nature of things this domination is in no way diminished today. In day-time the brooding magnificent shape of the mountain looms high over the surrounding countryside, and at night the explosive bursts of red-hot lava light up the sky - while in intervals between the fireworks, the dull glow of the molten lava is always visible.

Perhaps the best place from which to view Mount Etna is Taormina, as from here it makes a wonderful silhouette, especially in the evening sky with the light shining behind the majestic ascending slopes.

Figure 9 An extract from Anthony Pereira's writings on Sicily

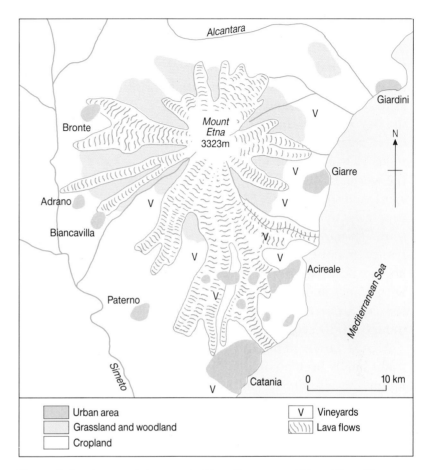

Urban area
Grassland and woodland
Cropland
V Vineyards
Lava flows

Figure 8 Land use and the extent of lava flows around Mount Etna. The fertile soils around Mount Etna are used for cultivating arable crops and vineyards. Grass and woodland alternate with lava flows on the higher slopes

Work Programme

- In pairs, make a list of the ways in which the natural features of the Mezzogiorno could be used to attract tourists into the area.
- With the aid of Figures 4 and 6, consider how Mount Vesuvius and Pompeii have already been developed as tourist attractions. How could tourism be developed further in these areas?
- Use Figure 8 to describe the land use on and around the slopes of Mount Etna.
- Draw a sketch map of this part of Sicily. Add labels to the map to show how you think it could be promoted as a tourist attraction.

8 The tourist potential

Italy is often described as the 'home of tourism'. Some places have been used as resorts for thousands of years, like the Bay of Naples and the island of Capri. At present, the Italian tourist industry is one of the most diverse in the world. It offers history, scenery, sport, and sun. In 1985, 53 million people visited the country, mainly from Germany, the USA, the UK, and France, making it one of the top three holiday destinations in Europe along with France and Spain. Indeed, foreign tourists are an essential source of money for the economy.

A great variety of holidays have traditionally been on offer in Italy. The mountains absorb one-third of the tourists, both for winter sports (especially skiing) and for stays in the Lake District around Lakes Como, Garda, and Maggiore. Other visitors choose coastal package tours to the Adriatic (Rimini, Cattolica, and Pesaro), Tuscany, and the North-East where there are many kilometres of broad, sandy beaches. Many Italians also use these resorts. The southern coast has been opened up to tourism by better road and rail links, but it has not developed in the same way. The third type of holiday for which Italy is famous is a city holiday. Italy has more listed historic monuments than any other country in the world, so large numbers of people visit cities such as Rome, Venice, and Florence to experience their culture. The cities of the South do not have the same cultural richness and so remain largely unexplored.

There are still many parts of the Italian landscape which remain undiscovered by tourists, and most of these are in the Mezzogiorno. The

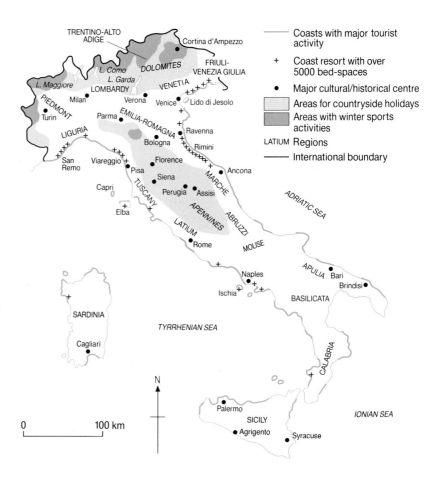

South cannot provide winter sports holidays and so has to rely on the summer season for its tourist trade. The image of the South as backward and depressed does not help to attract tourists. Many holidaymakers in the Mezzogiorno already live in the region and travel short distances to the nearest coastal or hill resort.

The greatest growth in Italy's tourist industry took place in the 1950s and 1960s and is now slowing down. In many areas there is no longer a need to build more large-scale facilities. But in the South there is room to develop small-scale activities spread throughout the region, such as coastal campsites.

Figure 1 Map showing tourist developments in Italy. There are few major coast resorts in the South

Tours of Italy

This magical country casts a spell on all who visit her. The unique combination of natural beauty and rich historical background makes people return year after year. The spirit of Italy is everywhere and above all in the relaxed, Italian way of life. Enjoy spending hours in the pavement cafés, watching the world go by or slowly taking the 'passegiata' - promenading along the main streets. Italy is a shopper's paradise with elegant designer-clothes, wonderful shoes and bags from each of the different regions. Most of all, sample the excellent food and try any of the local wine.

 **SCENIC CHARM**

The magnificent scenery of the Bay of Naples has attracted visitors for centuries. Breathtaking and beautiful, you can explore it with the benefit of a guide on an excursion or why not hire a car? The drive to Amalfi along the coast road is particularly spectacular and passes through delightful villages such as Positano. Or try catching a ferry to Capri where you'll find Roman ruins, beautiful villas and some of the most romantic scenery in the world.

Figure 2 The extracts are from tourist brochures. The photos show just two of the attractions of southern Italy: small harbours and traditional Sicilian villages

Activity

1 Using all the information on these pages and your work from the previous assignment, your task is to develop a tourist brochure for the Mezzogiorno. This should contain both written and illustrative materials which advertise tourist attractions and developments in the South. You may also find it useful to look in holiday brochures for places such as Sicily to see what tourist facilities exist at the moment and how these could be improved and expanded. Be careful to avoid changes which may highlight some of the disadvantages of tourism.

Tourism...
...may increase begging
...may lead to stress in agriculture whereby goods are produced for the tourist market, leaving production of staple foods short
...may place stresses on local customs

Figure 3 Cartoons warning of the problems that can be caused by tourism

1 Afon Conwy: from source to sea

Figure 1 Two views of the Afon Conwy

There is probably a river or a stream near where you live. It might be famous, like the River Clyde in Scotland, known around the world for the ships (like the QEII) that were built upon it. It might be big and powerful or it might be small and known only to the people who live near it. Whatever it is like, your local river or stream will be similar in many ways to the Afon Conwy in North Wales, the river used as the case study in this section about 'Rivers in the landscape'.

The Afon Conwy is only 35 km long. It flows from its source at Llyn Conwy, over 400 metres above sea-level, down to the Irish Sea between Conwy and the Great Ormes Head. The photographs in Figure 1 will give you an idea of the different types of landscape that can be found along its course. There are a lot of things which influence the landscapes and indeed the river itself along its course. The climate obviously has a big part to play. The types of rock and soil are also important. But perhaps one of the most important influences on the landscape are people – farmers, builders, and foresters. Try to think how each of these things influences the landscape and the river – are there any other things that have been left out?

Just as people have had an influence on rivers and their landscapes, it is true to say that these things have also affected people's lives. For example, the Afon Conwy is so wide where it enters the sea that specially designed and expensive bridges have had to be built to get from one bank to the other. Generally speaking, most people have adapted their lives so that they are in harmony with the river and its landscapes. Occasionally, things happen that disturb this harmony, sometimes with dreadful consequences – as we shall see later in this section.

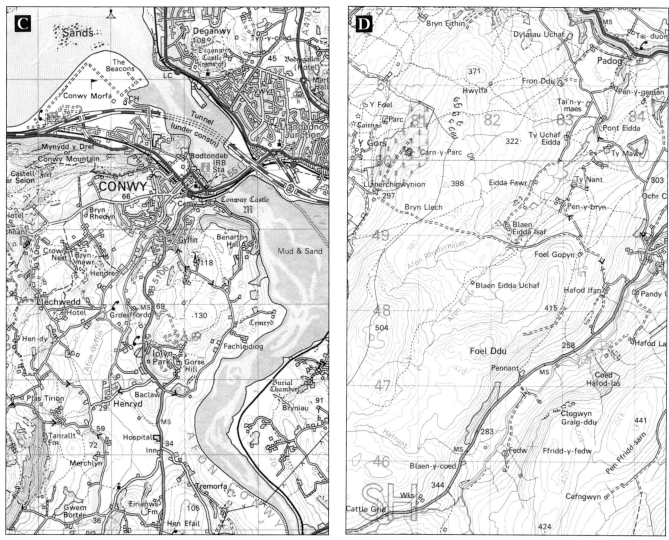

Figure 2 Ordnance Survey 1:50 000 map extracts showing sections of the Afon Conwy

Activities

1 The two photographs of the Afon Conwy in Figure 1 were taken in areas covered by the Ordnance Survey map extracts in Figure 2. Study the photographs and maps carefully.
a) Which map extract matches which photo?
b) In which direction was the camera pointing when Photo B was taken?
(Hint: try to find major landmarks on the photograph that you can also identify on the map extract.)

2 Study each of the two photo-map pairs. For each location, use the evidence to describe:
 – the nature of the river;
 – the major landscape features;
 – the land use of the area.

You may want to discuss this as a group before you write your own description.

3 Research idea:
Trace the route taken by your local river or stream as it flows from its source to the sea. What sort of landscapes can be found on its banks? How does the river itself change along its route? How do people make use of the river? There are lots of other questions that you can ask yourself. You might like to present your research as a large wall display or map, to be put on the wall of the classroom.

2 Rainfall into river

All water on the land eventually makes its way down to the sea, due to the force of gravity. Rivers are the main way in which it does this. But have you ever thought about what happens to precipitation once it has reached the ground, but before it gets into the river? Figure 1 shows that this is not as simple as it might seem.

The diagram shows that the precipitation can either become surface runoff and flow directly down to the river, or it can soak into the ground by a process called infiltration.

Even if the water has soaked into the ground, it still has different routes by which it could reach the river channel. It might go as throughflow, moving down the air space in the soil. This is much slower than surface runoff. Some water may percolate deep underground, into the bedrock. But this is only if the rock is permeable. Some rocks are impermeable and will not absorb water. The movement of water through the rock, called groundwater flow, is the slowest route that water can follow – it might take days or even weeks to reach the river.

By investigating the way in which water reaches the river channel, scientists (called hydrologists) can make it easier for people to live in harmony with a river. For example, a lot of quick surface runoff could mean that a river is more likely to flood. If there is no slow groundwater flow, because the rock is impermeable, the river could dry up in times of drought. If people change the way that they use the land drained by a river (its drainage basin), the routes taken by precipitation might change, affecting the balance or equilibrium between people and the river.

Figure 1 A hillslope diagram, with students doing an infiltration test

Fieldwork to find out more about infiltration

Equipment - What you will need
- infiltration tubes - could be made from large, catering-sized tin cans with the top and the bottom cut off or from a 40 cm length of big plastic pipe
- bucket and supply of water
- metre rule
- stopwatch

Method - What you do
1. Choose your sites (see Figure 3). Push your infiltration ring about 10 cm into the ground. Make sure that water can only escape by soaking into the ground.
2. Stand the metre rule in the ring.
3. Fill the tube to the top with water.
4. Wait one minute.
5. Measure and record the drop in the water level.
6. Refill the tube.
7. Wait another minute.
8. Measure drop in level.
9. Repeat for another five minutes.

Figure 2 Investigating infiltration

The information collected (*Results*)

The students in Figure 1 are carrying out an investigation into the infiltration rates on a hillside near the source of the Afon Conwy. They are measuring the rates of infiltration, using the method described in Figure 2, at three sites on the hillslope - how would you describe the locations of these sites? The results of their tests are given as follows.

Site	Drop in level of water at 1 minute intervals (mm)							Total drop in level
	1	1	1	1	1	1	1	
A	103	68	57	49	44	42	41	
B	52	43	37	34	31	29	25	
C	29	17	15	14	14	13	12	

Sorting out the results (*Analysis*)

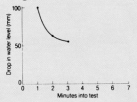

1. Make a copy of this graph.
2. Using three different colours, plot the results from the fieldwork onto the graph. Part of Site A has been done for you.
3. Label each of the lines according to the location of the site.

What has been found out? (*Conclusions*)

1. Write a brief description of each line that you have drawn on your graph.
2. What do they tell you about how infiltration rates vary according to where you are on the slope.
3. What happens to the infiltration rate after a long period of precipitation? Is surface runoff more likely in a long heavy rainstorm or a light drizzle?
4. What would the graphs have looked like on a steeper slope? Or a shallower slope?

Figure 3 Analysing the results of the infiltration test

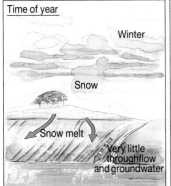

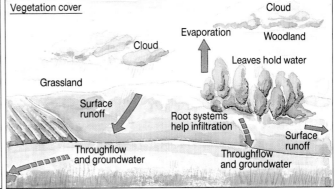

Figure 4 Factors influencing infiltration

Activities

1 In your own words, explain the difference between permeable and impermeable rocks. Try and find out some examples of each.

2 Carry out the analysis of the fieldwork results shown in Figure 3. Write a list of the conclusions that you reach.

3 Using your findings and Figure 4 to help you, explain what would be the consequences of doing the following in a river's drainage basin:

a) building a large new housing estate;

b) cutting down a large forest.

4 Fieldwork idea:
Carry out an investigation into infiltration rates in your school grounds. You will need to choose the test sites carefully, bearing in mind the factors that influence infiltration. Write up your findings using the headings given in Figures 2 and 3.

3 A rocky bed

Figure 1 Swallow Falls

The main job of a river is to move large quantities of water down to the sea. This is all part of the hydrological cycle. The Afon Conwy delivers millions of litres every day into the Irish Sea. But rivers also have another very important function in the landscape, as part of the rock cycle. If you look at Photo A in Figure 1 on page 54, you will see that the river is flowing at the bottom of a steep gorge. How did the gorge get there? The river has worn away or eroded the land and transported the fragments of rock, known as sediment, down towards the sea. Such erosion means that rivers sometimes look muddy, as they are transporting sediment.

Eventually, the sediment will be dropped by the river or carried out to sea. This process is called deposition.

All rivers erode the landscape, but some more than others. The Yellow River (Huang He) in China, for example, transports 1600 million tonnes of sediment every year. The Afon Conwy cannot live up to this, but still transports several thousand tonnes of sediment every year into the Irish Sea.

If you look at Photo A in Figure 1 on page 54 again, you will see that erosion by the river has left its mark on the landscape. For example, there is a lot of bare rock showing, and the slopes are all quite steep. Notice how all of the bare rock that you can see is smoothed and rounded, as if it had been rubbed with sandpaper. In effect that is exactly what the river has done to it. The sediment carried by the water has smoothed all the surfaces over which it has passed. This process is called abrasion. If you were to examine the river more closely, you would find that any loose stones or pebbles lying in the channel were also rounded. They too have been eroded, as they tumble along in the flow of water. This second type of erosion is called attrition. A few types of rocks (such as limestone) are soluble in water, and rivers dissolve the land away, by a process called corrosion.

The spectacular section of river in Figure 1 is known as Swallow Falls, on the Afon Llugwy, one of the tributaries or rivers that flow into the Afon Conwy. It is a very popular place with tourists. Swallow Falls have been created where the river crosses an area of harder rock, which cannot be eroded as easily as rock further downstream. Figure 2 gives more details of just how important Swallow Falls are as a tourist attraction in this part of North Wales.

Activities

1 In your own words, explain the different ways in which a river erodes the land.

2 On an outline map of the British Isles, draw bar charts or histograms to show were tourists visiting Swallow Falls have come from.

3 The questionnaire in Figure 2 does not find out all the information it could do. Add on another four or so questions that will investigate:
  – why the tourists come to Swallow Falls;
  – what they like and dislike;
  – what they would like to see improved;
  – anything else that you feel is important.

4 Why do you think that there is such an uneven distribution of tourists to Swallow Falls throughout the year?

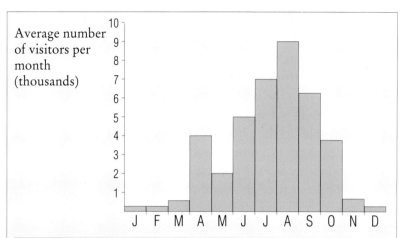

Average number of visitors per month (thousands)

% of tourists who visited Swallow Falls			
Region	%	Region	%
Wales	3	NE England	9
Scotland	5	The Midlands	27
Ireland	0	East Anglia	0
NW England	45	SE England	7
SW England	2	Other	2 (USA)

These figures were for one day in June 1989

Questionnaire

'Excuse me, we are doing some research work for a Geography project at school, and wondered if you would mind answering a few short questions...?'

1. In which of these regions do you live?

Wales	NE England
Scotland	The Midlands
Ireland	East Anglia
NW England	SE England, including London
SW England	Other (specify)....

2. How did you hear about Swallow Falls?

Tourist Information	Friends
Guide Book	Other (specify)....

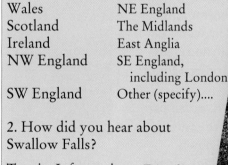

Figure 2 A data file on Swallow Falls. The photo shows tourists at the Miner's Bridge near Swallow Falls

4 Room to spread out

The photograph in Figure 1 was taken just a few miles from where the Afon Conwy flows into the sea. The landscape here is put to good use by the local people. In the photograph you will see that there is a wide expanse of flat land on either side of the river channel. This is called the flood plain. Figure 2 is a cross-section drawn across the valley and shows the flood plain quite clearly. What material is the flood plain made of? Small banks or levées on either side of the river are made naturally as the river deposits sediment near the channel when it floods. They are frequently made higher by people as a protection against floods. How would they stop flooding? Virtually all of the flood plain is used by local farmers, mainly for grazing their sheep and cattle. Why do you think so little of the flood plain is used for growing crops? Does the name 'flood plain' give you a clue?

The river itself is much wider here, over 200 metres wide where it enters the sea. It also winds from side to side across the flood plain, in big sweeping curves called meanders. The water is flowing smoothly, there are no rapids or waterfalls here. It is carrying a lot of sediment.

Because this part of the river is near to the sea, it is affected by the tides, and its level will go up and down accordingly. If you were to look closely at the river banks, you would see that they are made up of layer upon layer of sediment brought down by the river and deposited as alluvium to form the flood plain. This means that although erosion takes place along the entire length of a river, deposition is the main process as the river gets nearer to the sea. Figure 4 shows how a river

Figure 1 The lower Conwy Valley

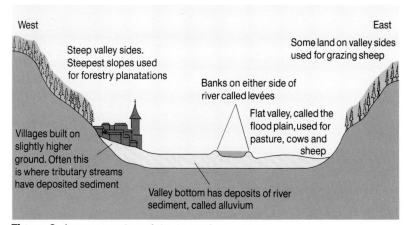

Figure 2 A cross-section of the lower Conwy Valley

feature called an ox-bow lake is formed when meanders become so tight that they 'meet' themselves. If you look closely at the large-scale map on the next page, you should be able to spot an ox-bow lake.

Figure 3 An unfinished sketch of Figure 1

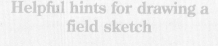

Helpful hints for drawing a field sketch

–Always draw a frame around your sketch.

–Try 'framing' the view with your hands before you begin.

–Start with the sky-line. Pay close attention to the angles of the horizon.

–Next draw any other 'major' lines in the view, i.e. river, railway, or outlines of hills.

–Identify major areas of vegetation, e.g. woodlands, fields, and so on.

–Show hillsides by line shading.

–Do not worry too much about detail, your labels (annotations) will help with that.

Figure 5

Figure 4 The formation of an ox-bow lake

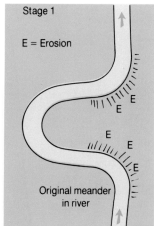
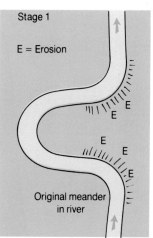

Stage 1

E = Erosion

Original meander in river

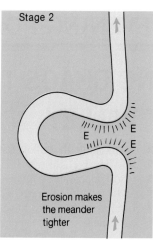

Stage 2

Erosion makes the meander tighter

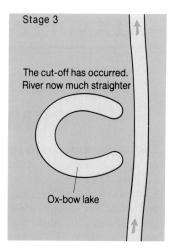

Stage 3

The cut-off has occurred. River now much straighter

Ox-bow lake

Activities

1 Make a full-sized copy of Figure 3. Remember the helpful hints that you have been given!

2 Draw more detail on to the sketch. This should include settlements, trees, fields, and anything else that you feel is important.

3 Annotate your field sketch or, in other words, put labels on to it. These labels serve two purposes:
a) to identify features in the landscape, like the name of a village;
b) to explain something about them, such as why the village is sited on slightly higher ground at the edge of the flood plain.

4 If you do not have enough room on your sketch, you could always write outside the sketch and then point to the feature with an arrow. You could use a key too!

5 Try your hand at completing another field sketch. Maybe you could draw the landscape that can be seen from your classroom or bedroom window.

5 Assignment: Flooding in Llanrwst

Background information

Like many rivers, the Afon Conwy sometimes overflows its banks and floods the surrounding land. The information on these pages is about a flood event.

Your assignment

Your task is to find out what happened and why, and to think about ways to reduce the impact of flooding on people's lives.

Figure 1 (right) Receding flood-waters around Llanrwst, in the lower Conwy Valley

Friday 26 April

LLANDUDNO EVENING POST

FLOODS BRING CHAOS TO CONWY VALLEY

Last night, widespread flooding occurred in the valley of the Afon Conwy. The area around Llanrwst was the worst hit. Police and volunteers with boats worked throughout the night to move people to safety. Mrs Agnes Jones (27) had to be flown by a helicopter from RAF Valley to Llandudno General Hospital after going into premature labour.

Farmers had to work hard to save their animals, and even so many are feared drowned. Homes and buildings in Llanrwst, including factories on the Station Industrial Estate, were inundated by flood waters, causing thousands of pounds worth of damage. Insurance assessors have promised that they will visit the area tomorrow. Several roads have been closed by the flooding, including the B5106 which is still impassable between Llanrwst and Trefriw. All weekend football fixtures in the valley have had to be cancelled.

The floods are already beginning to recede, leaving a fine layer of mud over everything. They come at the end of a period of very wet weather and were the direct result of nearly 20 mm of rain in the last 48 hours. The river rose and burst its banks very quickly, and there was little time to issue a flood warning.

Figure 2 Newspaper extract

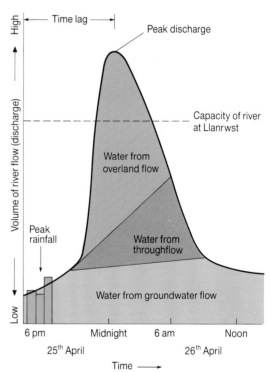

Figure 3 What happens when a river floods?

The amount of water moving down a river is called the **discharge**. It is the key to understanding what happens in a flood. A river channel can only hold so much discharge, so if the river has more water than this it will burst its banks and flood. This graph shows what happened on the morning of 26th April. It is called a **hydrograph**.

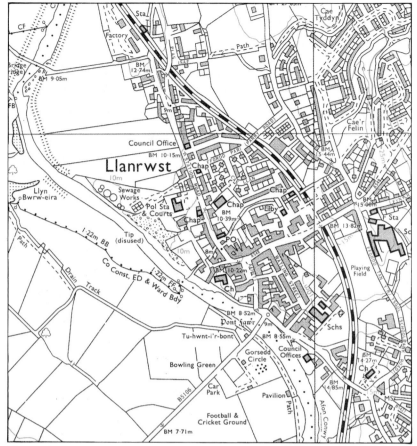

Figure 4 Llanrwst, from an Ordnance Survey 1:10 000 map

WHAT CAN BE DONE TO REDUCE THE IMPACT OF FLOODS ?

LAND USE CONTROLS
Do not use land that often floods

FLOOD WARNING SYSTEMS
Hydrologists can now better predict floods

HOLD IT BACK!
Keep water in upper part of drainage basin, either by
building dams or planting trees

KEEP WATER IN!
Make river deeper by dredging, or build flood barriers
along river banks

GET RID OF IT!
Straighten river channels to improve flow, or build new
channels to divert flood water away from danger areas

Figure 5 Ways of controlling the impact of floods

Work Programme A

1 What Happened?
Study Figure 3.
● At what time did the flooding start
  at Llanrwst?
● How long did it last?
● How much time was there between
  the peak rainfall and the peak
  discharge? This is called the lag
  time. How might this explain the
  difficulty of giving a warning of the
  flood?

2 What were the causes of the flood?
The newspaper article mentions three
possible causes of flooding:
  1 the very wet period of weather
     leading up to the floods;
  2 nearly 20 millimetres of rainfall in
     48 hours directly before the flood;
  3 cutting down trees in the upper
     drainage basin.
● Using the information in the 'Rivers
  in the landscape' section, suggest
  how each of these things might
  have caused the flood. Are there any
  other possible causes?

Work Programme B

1 What impact did the flood have?
● Draw a simple outline map of the
  area shown in Figure 4 showing:
    – the river;
    – the main roads and railway;
    – the main built up area.
● Write labels on your map to show
  what the main effects of the flood
  were on Llanrwst and the
  surrounding area. You should use
  the information in Figure 2 to help
  you. Do the contour lines help?

*2 What could be done to reduce the
impact of future floods?*
● Look at Figure 5. Can you think of
  ways in which any of these
  measures could be used at
  Llanrwst? Think of a way you can
  present your ideas.

6 *Comparing rivers*

Figure 1 The River Rhine (top) and the River Nile (bottom)

How many uses can you think of for rivers? Or the water in them? The photographs in Figure 1 should give you an idea of just how many uses there are. Rivers are very important to people. In fact many early civilisations grew up along rivers. One example was the Ancient Egyptian civilisation on the banks of the River Nile.

Our modern world could not exist without rivers either. Figure 2 gives information about how two of the world's major rivers are used. It also shows that using rivers often causes problems. These problems may result just in inconvenience, but frequently they cause great damage or even loss of life.

Whatever the problems, the fact is we need rivers. So we should be doing all we can to solve the problems that we have caused.

RIVER RHINE

Background Information

- 40 million people live in drainage basin
- Covers five countries
- River is 1200 km long
- Provides drinking water for 20 million people (most in Netherlands)
- 70% of German industry near River Rhine

Water Transport

- 257 million tonnes of cargo carried along Rhine in 1986
- Mainly bulk cargoes by barges up to 5000 tonnes - ores 18%, coal 9%
- Linked to rest of Europe's rivers and canals
- Rotterdam to Basle takes 6-7 days

Pollution

- Last salmon caught in 1950
- River stinks at low water levels
- Untreated sewage
- Thermal pollution
- In 1982, it contained high levels of mercury (3.9 tonnes) and phosphorus (37 000 tonnes) as well as arsenic, lead, and cadmium
- Long term issue
- Attempts have been made to clean it up

RIVER NILE

Background Information

- Longest river in the world, 6695 km long
- White Nile rises in Lake Victoria
- Main tributary is the Blue Nile
- Flows through four countries
- Over 50 million people live in drainage basin

Irrigation (after 1971)

- Cultivated area doubled
- Water available all year
- No more natural silt for fields so fertiliser has to be bought
- More stagnant water so more disease, e.g. bilharzia
- Few crops grown for local people, most exported

Aswan High Dam

- Completed in 1971
- Funded by Soviet Union
- Created Lake Nasser, as big as England
- People made homeless
- River navigable all year
- Floods controlled
- Fishing industry created
- Dam a tourist attraction
- Twice as much HEP as before

Figure 2 Facts and figures about the Rhine and the Nile

Activities

1 a) Make a large copy of this table.

Use of rivers	Problems caused by this use	Example

b) Work with a partner. Make a list of all the uses of rivers in column 1 on the table.

c) Complete the other two columns of the table. Not all uses cause problems, but many do if you really think about it.

2 How much of your completed table is true of the Afon Conwy?

3 Design a poster alerting people to the problems that face our rivers, and what they can do to help.

4 Research idea:
Find out who has the responsibility for looking after the rivers in your area. What problems do they have to solve? How might they do this?

1 Contrasts across the country

Have you ever lived in a different part of the country to where you live now? Have any of your family or friends? Even if you have answered 'no' to both these questions, you probably know that the way people live varies greatly from one part of Britain to another. Life in London, for example, is very different from life on a small farm in Yorkshire. People's homes, the jobs that they do, the way the land is used, and the services that are available can all vary in different parts of the country.

Figure 1 Contrasting scenes in different parts of the UK: a hill farmer checking his flock and rail commuters in the London rush hour

We have seen that it is quite easy to talk about and describe variations in life-style from one area to another. But sometimes we want to know more precisely about these variations. To do this we need to measure or quantify them. Planners, for example, need to know this information. Figure 2 is a map of the economic planning regions of the UK. Information or statistics about these regions is given in Figure 3. Much of this information is collected by a census. These are held every ten years, during the first year of the decade (1971, 1981, 1991 and so on). A census is when the government asks people questions about many aspects of their life-style, ranging from the job that they do, to what they do in their spare time. This information is confidential and only published in terms of the whole region, and not for individual families or households.

Figure 2 The Standard Planning Regions of the UK

Standard Planning Region	Population 000s 1981	% Population change 1971-81	% Workforce in manufacturing 1985	% Unemployment 1985	Number of cars per 1000 people 1991	Number of superstores 1986	% Land use Farm	% Land use Forest	% Land use Other
North	3097	-1.4	29	18.5	231	19	63	16	21
Yorks & Humberside	4854	-0.1	31	14.6	264	21	64	10	31
East Midlands	3807	4.8	34	12.4	301	20	80	4	16
East Anglia	1856	11.7	25	10.3	312	6	81	7	12
South-East	16729✳	-1.2	27	9.6	342	41	59	11	30
South-West	4326	6.0	24	11.3	298	17	77	9	14
West Midlands	5136	0.5	38	15.1	274	24	75	7	18
North-West	6406	-2.0	30	15.9	257	47	58	9	33
London	6696	-10.1	◆	◆	261	52	◆	◆	◆
Wales	2790	2.2	21	16.3	317	16	70	6	14
Scotland	5117	-2.1	22	15.3	268	31	71	16	13

✳ Including London   ◆ Included in South-East figure

Figure 3 Variations in how we live

Choropleth maps

If you look in an atlas, you will see that it is full of choropleth or shading maps.

ADVANTAGES
- They look good
- Easy to see overall patterns
- Quite easy to draw
- Can be used to highlight certain things
- Can be used for total numbers, but best for percentages

DISADVANTAGES
- Cannot be used to read actual figures from, only the range
- Cannot be used for all data
- Easy to give a false impression
- Looks dreadful if drawn incorrectly

RULES FOR CHOROPLETH MAPPING

- Do not use too many categories. Four or five is usually plenty
- Decide if highest or lowest figures more important, and use darkest colours for them
- Always use different shades of the same colour
- The interval (size) of categories must always be the same, e.g. 0-10, 11-20, 21-30, not 0-7, 8-11, 12-23
- Be aware of need to fit all the figure in, e.g. in 0-10, 11-20, where would you put 10.5?

Figure 4 Skills box: Choropleth (shading) maps

Activities

1 Make a list of ten ways in which people's lifestyle can vary from one part of Britain to another.

2 Study Figure 3. Which of the columns of information was collected by a census? For each of the other columns, suggest how the information might have been collected.

3 Read the information in Figure 4 about drawing choropleth or shading maps. Make a list of which of the columns of information in Figure 3 would be suitable for showing in a choropleth map. Compare your list with your neighbour.

4 Make a large copy of Figure 2. Choose one of the columns of data and plot it on the map that you have drawn as a choropleth map. Do not forget to give the map a title and a key.

5 Write a short paragraph to describe the pattern that is shown by your map. Is it what you expected? Compare it with your neighbour's map.

2 *Welcome to Sheffield*

Figure 1 An aerial view of part of Sheffield

What do you know about Sheffield? It is a city that is famous for many reasons: steelmaking, a university, a polytechnic, plenty of good shops, two football teams, snooker tournaments at the Crucible Theatre, and lots more.

Sheffield is the fourth-largest city in England, with 560 000 people. These people live in a wide variety of homes, some of which you can see in Figure 1. There are big blocks of flats built in the 1960s, rows of nineteenth century houses, large estates of 1930s council houses, detached suburban houses, and many others.

The city first grew in the valley where the River Sheaf (from which Sheffield gets its name) meets the River Don. It has for a long time been an industrial area, for the reasons given in Figure 4. It grew very quickly in the eighteenth and nineteenth centuries, along the river valleys and onto the nearby hillsides.

For a long time, steelmaking was the main industry in the city (see Figure 4). But other countries started making steel more cheaply, and Sheffield's factories started closing down. This has left Sheffield with a lot of derelict land, areas where there is no work and where nature is slowly taking over. Sheffield City Council is working hard to do something about these problems.

Figure 2 A map of Sheffield

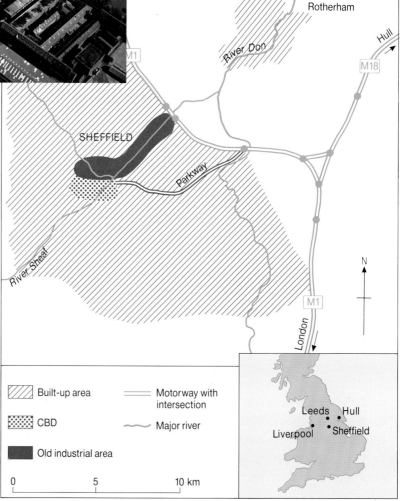

▨ Built-up area	═ Motorway with intersection	
▨ CBD	〰 Major river	
▮ Old industrial area		

0   5   10 km

On Sheffield's Doorstep

People in Sheffield have one of the most beautiful parts of England on their doorstep - the Peak District National Park. It offers countless leisure opportunities, ranging from a quiet walk to hang gliding. People like the area so much that the lucky ones now live in the Park and commute to work in Sheffield. The Peak District is also the source of Sheffield's water supply, and as the city's thirst grows, so do the calls to flood more land to create new reservoirs.

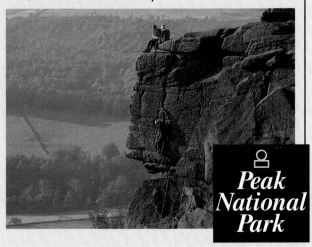

Well-dressing, a thanksgiving for water, is a popular tradition.

The dipper is often seen on fast-flowing rivers.

Walkers enjoy the view from the Kinder plateau.

Mountain Pansy, seen here in its yellow form.

Walking is the number one outdoor activity for visitors to the Peak National Park, and with 5,000 miles of public footpaths and 76 square miles of open access country, there are plenty of opportunities. The gritstone edges and limestone dales are favourite haunts for rock climbers, while the White Peak also attracts cavers who explore the unseen world of the underground.

Many visitors come to the Park to admire the pretty villages, many of which keep alive ancient traditions such as well-dressing. Others are attracted by the astonishing variety of wildlife in the Park. Many rarities are found here, including some northern species at their southern limit, and southern species at their northern extreme.

Peak National Park

Figure 3 'On Sheffield's doorstep'. Climbers in the Peak District, Derbyshire, and an extract from a Peak National Park tourist leaflet

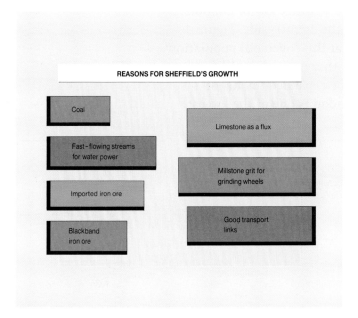

REASONS FOR SHEFFIELD'S GROWTH

- Coal
- Fast-flowing streams for water power
- Imported iron ore
- Blackband iron ore
- Limestone as a flux
- Millstone grit for grinding wheels
- Good transport links

Figure 4 Reasons for Sheffield's growth as an industrial centre

Activities

1 Sheffield is the fourth-largest city in England. Use your atlas to find out which cities have more people. Are there any larger cities in Scotland, Wales, or Ireland?

2 On a map of the British Isles, mark the location of these large cities. Try and find out what each of them is famous for. Write it on the map.

3 Look carefully at Figure 4, which shows some things which have been important for Sheffield. Using an atlas, find out where each of them came from. Which are still important? Show your answers on a large copy of Figure 4.

3 Welcome to Swindon

Figure 1 Swindon: the pool at the Oasis Leisure Centre and the Brunel Shopping Centre

Things are changing in Swindon. It is one of the most successful towns in the country. Lots of varied, new businesses have set up in Swindon in recent years. Many modern homes have been built, and the town's shopping and leisure facilities are some of the best to be found anywhere in Britain.

The town's success is due largely to its accessibility. By this we mean the fact that it is easy to get from Swindon to most other places in Britain. The map in Figure 2 shows that the town is linked to the motorway network by the M4, and is on the InterCity 125 railway line from Bristol to London. The town can be said to lie in a 'corridor of good accessibility'.

There are about 130 000 people living in Swindon today, compared with just 65 000 in 1945. Most of this growth was planned to house people who wanted to move out of London and live in the countryside. Figure 4 explains that this 'overspill population' moved to either new towns like Bracknell, or expanded towns, of which Swindon is one of the largest.

Figure 2 The M4 corridor

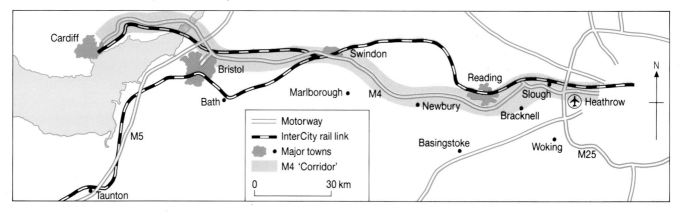

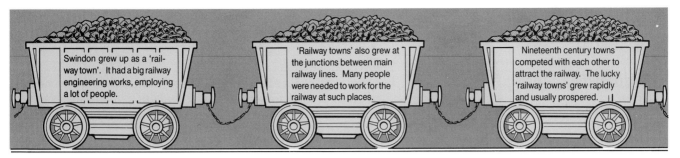

Swindon grew up as a 'railway town'. It had a big railway engineering works, employing a lot of people.

'Railway towns' also grew at the junctions between main railway lines. Many people were needed to work for the railway at such places.

Nineteenth century towns competed with each other to attract the railway. The lucky 'railway towns' grew rapidly and usually prospered.

Figure 3 Railway towns

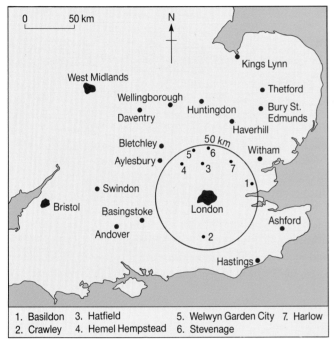

1. Basildon   3. Hatfield   5. Welwyn Garden City   7. Harlow
2. Crawley   4. Hemel Hempstead   6. Stevenage

Figure 4 New and expanded towns in South-East England

Figure 5 The growing populations of the new and expanded towns in South-East England

---

Activities

1 In your own words, explain what is meant by the term 'accessibility'.

2 a) Make a copy of the table on the right.
b) Using an atlas, measure the distance by motorway from Swindon to the cities given. Fill in your findings.

3 a) Working with a partner, decide on the average speed of motorway travel
(i) by car   (ii) by lorry.
b) Calculate the travel time distances from Swindon and fill in your findings on your table.

4 Write about the reasons for building new and expanded towns, and where they can be found in South-East England.

City	Motorway distance from Swindon	Motorway time distance from Swindon	
		Car	Lorry
LONDON			
SHEFFIELD			
BRISTOL			
CARDIFF			
LIVERPOOL			
EXETER			
DOVER*			
CARLISLE			
GLASGOW*			
BIRMINGHAM			
NEWCASTLE*			

* Includes some non-motorway

71

4 Job prospects

Reg Morrell's Story

'I've lived in Sheffield all my life. Left school at 14, and went to work in a steelworks. It was hard work, dirty, very physical, rolling the metal into sheets. The company had 100 workers, and we made <u>high quality stainless steel</u> which was sent all over the world.

The works closed down in 1973. We were told that foreign steel was <u>undercutting the market</u>. I was unemployed for a while, but I'm skilled, so I got a job in the end. It's a smaller place, only six of us, cleaner too. We make stainless steel fittings using steel imported from Sweden!

Lots of the new jobs in Sheffield are like mine - small firms, using <u>skilled workers</u>. My brother isn't skilled like me. He has <u>temporary jobs</u>, on building sites, but then gets <u>laid off</u> when the job's done.'

Jane Norris's Story

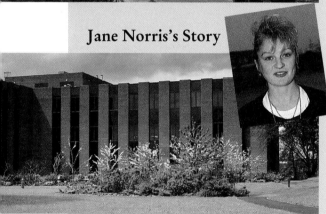

'I've had quite a few jobs since I left school, there's no shortage of work here. Now I'm with an electronics firm, making <u>components</u> for TVs. It's highly skilled, and I've been on courses to get more <u>experience</u> and <u>qualifications</u>. I work on a <u>production line</u>. The <u>working conditions</u> are good, I'm well paid, and there are lots of <u>fringe benefits</u>.

The factory is right next to the M4. It is very accessible. It was built by the local authority. The boss says it would have cost twice as much to set up in London. My sister <u>commutes</u> to London every day. My dad is retired now, but he used to work in the British Rail works here, before it closed.'

Figure 1

What type of job?

There are hundreds of different jobs that people do, but they can be divided (classified) into three groups or sectors.

Primary industries are those which produce raw materials from the land or sea, e.g. fishing, mining, farming, forestry.

Farmer

Secondary industries manufacture things from the raw materials, or process them, e.g. steelmaking, car manufacturing, food processing.

Car Worker

Tertiary industries provide a service to people or the community, e.g. salesman, teacher, lorry driver, policewoman.

Nurse

The number of people in each of these three groups varies from one part of the country to another, as shown in this table.

	% of the workforce in each group		
	Primary	Secondary	Tertiary
SHEFFIELD	15	51	34
SWINDON	2	31	67
UNITED KINGDOM	2	34	64

Figure 2

Pie Charts

Most atlases have lots of pie charts (or pie graphs) in them. They are usually used to show the proportion of things that make up a total. For example, the proportion of an area used for farming, forestry, towns, or other uses. The data needed is normally in the form of percentages.

If you follow these steps, it is quite easy to draw a pie chart. You will need
- a calculator
- a pair of compasses
- a ruler
- a protractor
- a pencil and coloured pencils

In this example, the data is the percentages of people in Sheffield who work in the different sectors of industry.

Step 1

Work out how big each slice of pie, or segment, should be.

The whole circle represents 100% and measures 360° around.

Therefore 1% would be $\frac{360°}{100} = 3.6°$

$15\% = 15 \times 3.6° = 54°$

Now copy and complete this table:

	Primary		Secondary		Tertiary	
	%	Angle	%	Angle	%	Angle
Sheffield	15	54°	51	184°	34	
Swindon						
United Kingdom						

Step 2
Draw a circle. Draw a line at 12 o'clock.

Step 3
Measure the angle of the first segment, going clockwise from 12 o'clock and draw a line.

54°

Step 4
Add the next segment. This time measure clockwise from the last line that you drew.

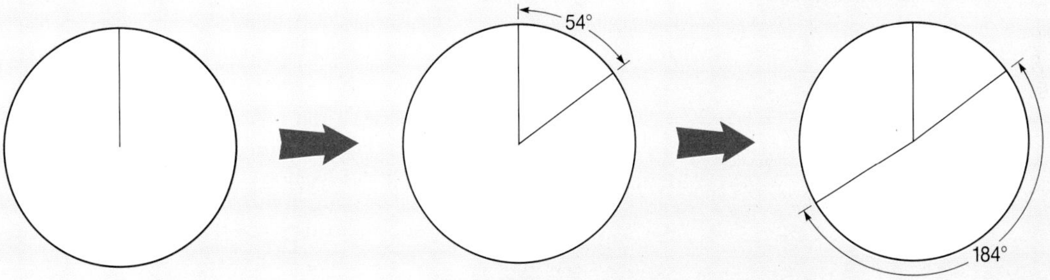

184°

Step 5
Colour the pie chart. Add a key and title to explain what it shows.

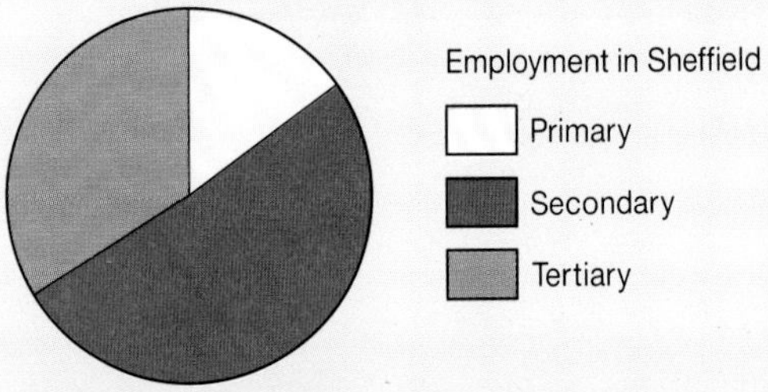

Employment in Sheffield
- Primary
- Secondary
- Tertiary

Figure 3 Skills box: Pie charts

Activities

1 Working as a group, discuss what the words and phrases mean that are underlined in the two stories in Figure 1. Compare your ideas with the rest of the class. Write a 'definition' of each word or phrase for your own use.

2 The stories tell you what Reg and Jane's families do for a living. Which sectors of industry do they work in? Use Figure 2 to help you decide. Design a table to show your answers.

3 The skills box shows you how to draw pie charts. Draw your own pie charts for the information in Figure 2.

4 Research idea:
What sort of job would you like to do when you leave school? In which sector of industry is it? What about the rest of the class? And families/friends? Design and carry out a survey to find out.

5 Home sweet home

What sort of home do you have? Is it old or new, a house or a flat, built of bricks or stone? Whatever it is like, there are probably homes very similar to yours in both Swindon and Sheffield. Some types of home will be more common in one place than another. This section investigates some of the homes that are common in Swindon and Sheffield.

Figure 1 Housing types in Sheffield and Swindon

SHEFFIELD

The photo shows some of Sheffield's old terraced houses and some of the city's tower blocks.

The terraced houses were built up to 200 years ago for the thousands of new factory workers. They were built in long rows close to the factories. They were small and poorly built— some even fell down!

During the 1950s and 1960s, the council pulled down many of the old terraced houses (those that remain have been modernised). Large blocks of flats were built in their place. The flats were cheap and quick to build and provided modern amenities, like bathrooms, that the old houses did not have. Children could play on the open spaces between the blocks.

However, most people now agree that the tower blocks have been a failure. They were poorly built and needed frequent repairs. Crime became a big problem. People hated living in them. Many of the flats are now empty and boarded up and the remaining residents want to move somewhere else.

SWINDON

Swindon has a wide range of house types, including some old terraced houses. But many of the homes in the town are quite modern, like those in the photo.

Swindon has grown rapidly in recent years and several large housing estates have been built on the edge of the town. On these estates you can find a mixture of house types. Modern terraced, semi-detached, and detached houses are all within a short distance of each other. Most have a garden and a garage, and most have central heating and good insulation.

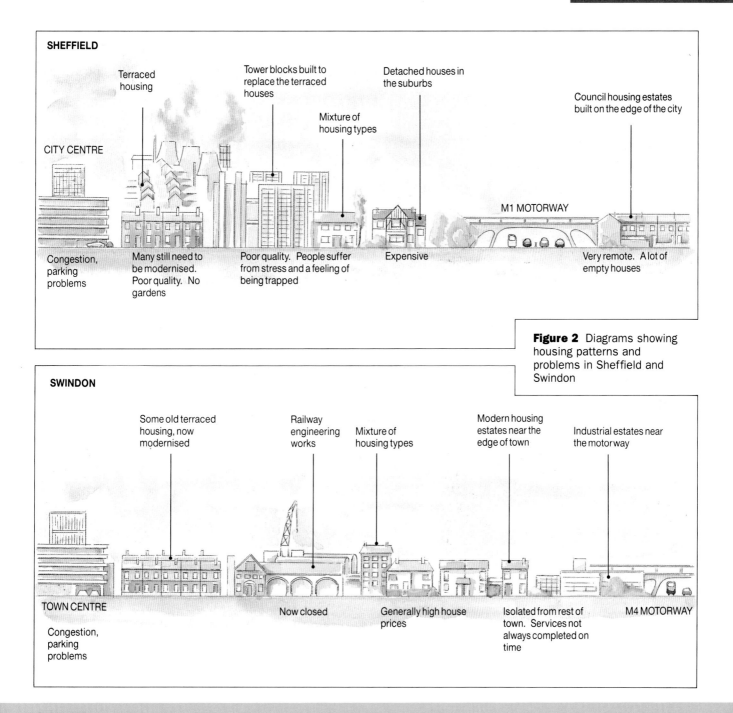

SHEFFIELD

Terraced housing

Tower blocks built to replace the terraced houses

Detached houses in the suburbs

Mixture of housing types

Council housing estates built on the edge of the city

CITY CENTRE

M1 MOTORWAY

Congestion, parking problems

Many still need to be modernised. Poor quality. No gardens

Poor quality. People suffer from stress and a feeling of being trapped

Expensive

Very remote. A lot of empty houses

Figure 2 Diagrams showing housing patterns and problems in Sheffield and Swindon

SWINDON

Some old terraced housing, now modernised

Railway engineering works

Mixture of housing types

Modern housing estates near the edge of town

Industrial estates near the motorway

TOWN CENTRE

M4 MOTORWAY

Congestion, parking problems

Now closed

Generally high house prices

Isolated from rest of town. Services not always completed on time

Activities

1 Each of the housing types mentioned in Figure 1 were built for different reasons. What were those reasons?

2 Think about the things that are similar and different when comparing housing in Swindon and Sheffield. Make two lists - one for similarities and the other for differences.

3 Housing that people will like living in needs careful planning and designing. Working as a small group, decide upon a list of things that

planners should consider when building an area of new housing.

4 Imagine that you live in either Swindon or Sheffield, in one of the areas mentioned in Figure 1. Write a short story about your life there. What are the people like? What do they do? What are the houses like? Are there any problems? Use as much information from this section of the book as you can.

6 Assignment: Environmental quality

Background information

The houses in Figures 1 and 2 might look similar at first glance. But look more closely. The environment in Figure 1 is of a much higher quality than that shown in Figure 2. How many differences in environmental quality can you find between the areas shown in Figures 1 and 2?

Figure 1 (below left)

Figure 2

Method 1 : Housing Survey

This survey is to help you find out about the typical housing in an area. Firstly, decide on a house that is typical of the area.

1. Write a short description of the house.

2. Make a sketch of the house.

3. How many bedrooms do you think the house has?

4. How wide is the 'plot' of the house?

5. How deep is the plot?

6. How big is the plot in square metres?

7. Estimate value of the house. (Look in an estate agents to help you.)

How does this method show environmental quality?

Your assignment

Your task is to find out about differences like these in the area where you live. You are aiming to discover how the environmental quality varies from one place to another. It is up to you to decide exactly what you are going to investigate. Some ideas for ways of investigating environmental quality are outlined here. You can add your own ideas, too. Perhaps as part of your investigation, you will be able to suggest ways of improving areas of poor environmental quality. If you live in a rural area, you might want to do this work in your local town. You should choose at least four different areas within your local environment and investigate each.

Method 2 : Transport Survey

1. How busy is the street? (Count the number of vehicles passing you in a 5-minute period.)
2. Is there a speed limit? YES/NO. If yes, what is it?
3. Is there any public transport? YES/NO. If yes, how frequent is it?
4. Is there any off-road parking? YES/NO. If yes, how much?

- A busy street has a lower environmental quality than a quiet one.
- A speed limit also means a better environment.
- Public transport gives local people the chance not to use their cars.
- Off-road parking makes for a better environment.

Method 3 : Environmental Survey

In this method you give the area a mark for various aspects of the environment. The higher the mark, the better the environmental quality.

Feature of the environment	Very Good ◄——————— Mark ———————► Very Bad				
	5	4	3	2	1
State of repair of road/pavement					
State of repair of houses					
Amount of street lighting					
General tidiness					
Amount of litter					
Total mark for area			/25 (highest possible mark)		

Method 4 : Personal Evaluation

This method is to give the area a value in terms of how it 'feels' to you. Once again you give the area a mark according to which words best describe the area. The higher the total mark the better the environmental quality.

Interesting	5	4	3	2	1	Boring
Bright	5	4	3	2	1	Dull
Quiet	5	4	3	2	1	Noisy
Safe	5	4	3	2	1	Unsafe
Pretty	5	4	3	2	1	Ugly
Clean	5	4	3	2	1	Dirty
Total mark for area	/25 (highest possible mark)					

Writing up your investigation

Your investigation should be written up using the following headings:

- Aims - what you set out to investigate;
- Methods - how you collected the information (refer to Methods 1-4);
- Results - the information that you collected;
- Conclusions - what you discovered.

77

1 What is development?

We live in a world that is divided between the rich and the poor, the hungry and the well-fed, the sheltered and the homeless. Some parts of the world are noticeably richer than other parts. In fact, one line is often drawn on the map to divide the world into its richer and poorer parts (Figure 1).

The 'North' is described as being developed. The countries of the North are wealthy. They have a high level of industrial development and most of the population have a good standard of living. The United States of America, the UK, and Japan are all 'developed' countries.

The 'South' is described as developing. The countries of the South are poorer, in comparison with the north. Many of the people living in the South gain their living by farming. For many people the standard of living is low. Ethiopia, Brazil, and India, although very different as countries, are all in what is called the South.

Figure 1 A divided world. Statistics about each of the countries labelled on this map are given in Figure 2

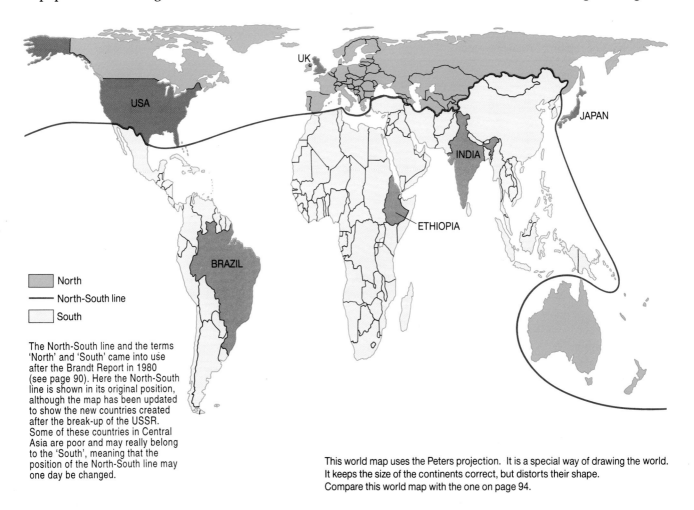

Legend:
- North
- North-South line
- South

The North-South line and the terms 'North' and 'South' came into use after the Brandt Report in 1980 (see page 90). Here the North-South line is shown in its original position, although the map has been updated to show the new countries created after the break-up of the USSR. Some of these countries in Central Asia are poor and may really belong to the 'South', meaning that the position of the North-South line may one day be changed.

This world map uses the Peters projection. It is a special way of drawing the world. It keeps the size of the continents correct, but distorts their shape. Compare this world map with the one on page 94.

INDICATORS OF DEVELOPMENT	UK	USA	JAPAN	ETHIOPIA	BRAZIL	INDIA
GDP PER CAPITA (US $) The earnings of the country divided by the number of people.	10120	18848	19464	104	2115	283
LIFE EXPECTANCY (years) The age people are expected to live to.	74.4	75	77.2	41.9	64.9	57.9
LITERACY (%) The percentage of the adult population that can read and write.	99	99	99	35	79	36
URBAN POPULATION (%) The percentage of the population that live in towns and cities.	92	74	77	12	75	27
FOOD SUPPLY Number of calories per person per day.	3218	3642	2858	2110	2643	2204
DOCTOR: PATIENT RATIO Number of patients per doctor	1:680	1:470	1:660	1:77360	1:1080	1:2520

Figure 2 Some indicators of development. A photo from each of these countries is shown on the next page

Activities

1 Draw up a table with two columns. Head one of the columns 'Developed Country' and the other 'Developing Country'. Decide which of the following phrases would best describe the standard of living in each country, and write the phrase in the correct column.

Poor housing
Fewer chances for education
Most jobs in agriculture
Poorer diets
Well-fed
Most people live in cities
More chances for education
Most jobs in industry
Fewer medical care facilities
Most people live in the countryside
Good housing
More medical care

2 Look at the map (Figure 1). Using the map on page 94, name five countries that are in the 'North' and five countries that are in the 'South', other than those countries already labelled.

3 The information in Figure 2 compares six countries. Six indicators of development are used.
a) Choose three of the indicators which best show the differences in the level of development. Draw a graph for each set of the figures you have chosen.
b) Using your graphs, decide which of the countries is the most developed. Then draw up a rank order (list) from most to least developed country.
c) What other statistics, that are not shown in the table, would be good indicators of development?

4 Why are some countries more 'developed' than others?

Figure 3 Six photos showing contrasts in development around the world

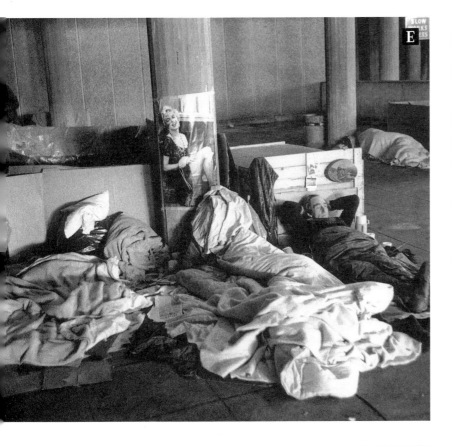

The photographs paint a confusing picture because they show that in many cases there are not big differences between the look of a developed or developing country. How then can we decide whether a country is developed or developing?

There are certain statistics that are good 'indicators of development'. They can show how wealthy a county is, and how good the average standard of living is for the people.

For a country to develop it needs to earn more money. This money can then be spent on better housing, education, and medical services for the population.

Money is earned by selling goods to other countries. These goods may be unprocessed, such as coffee beans. However, more money is made from selling processed goods, such as a jar of coffee granules.

To develop, therefore, a country needs to establish industries to process raw materials and produce manufactured goods.

2 Brazil: a developing country?

LOG'EM AND LEAVE'EM

BRAZIL DEBT CRISIS

LANDSLIDES KILL 277 PEOPLE IN RIO'S SHANTY TOWNS

THE RAVAGED RAINFOREST

THE LARGEST H.E.P STATION IN THE WORLD OPENS

Figure 1 How Brazil has hit the headlines

Brazil is often in the news. As you can see from the headlines, the news is often bad rather than good. The Amazon rainforest is perhaps the most common subject for news stories, because its possible destruction will affect us all. Scientists believe that the cutting down of the rainforest is a major contributor to the greenhouse effect.

Brazil is also famous for other things. Coffee, football, and carnival are just three images that often come to mind when you think of Brazil. These images do not necessarily suggest a picture of a developing country. As you will have seen from the indicators of development on page 79, it is difficult to label Brazil as either developed or developing. There are many people in Brazil who are wealthy and have a good standard of living. However, there is a far greater number whose standard of living is poor.

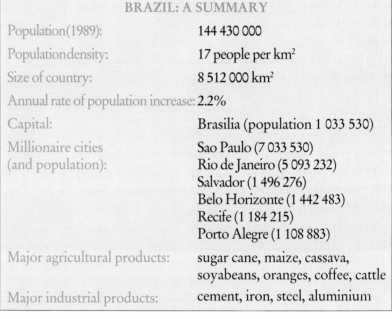

BRAZIL: A SUMMARY	
Population(1989):	144 430 000
Population density:	17 people per km²
Size of country:	8 512 000 km²
Annual rate of population increase:	2.2%
Capital:	Brasilia (population 1 033 530)
Millionaire cities (and population):	Sao Paulo (7 033 530) Rio de Janeiro (5 093 232) Salvador (1 496 276) Belo Horizonte (1 442 483) Recife (1 184 215) Porto Alegre (1 108 883)
Major agricultural products:	sugar cane, maize, cassava, soyabeans, oranges, coffee, cattle
Major industrial products:	cement, iron, steel, aluminium

Figure 2 Facts and figures about Brazil

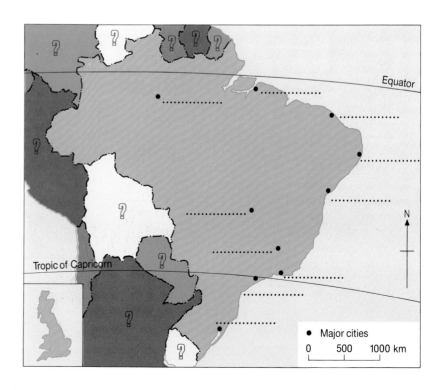

Figure 3 A map of Brazil (with Britain drawn to the same scale). For use with Activities 1-3

A LAND OF CONTRASTS

'I'm Isobella and I live in Sao Paulo with my husband and two children. My husband works for one of the big city banks and earns a good wage. Our apartment is close to the city centre. Security is very important, and there are checks made on everyone who arrives at the apartment block. The apartment is fairly large - a lounge, dining room, study, kitchen, four bedrooms and two bathrooms. We have lots of modern conveniences like a washing machine, television, video and stereo system, and we own two cars. A maid helps me out with the cleaning and cooking so that I have more time to spend with my children. The eldest attends a private school in the city. We usually manage to get away for a holiday every year, sometimes to the Brazilian coast, and occasionally abroad.'

Isobella's apartment

Maria's house

'Hello, my name is Maria, and I live on the outskirts of Sao Paulo in a slum district known as a favela. I have eight children who range in age from 6 months to 17 years old. My husband is a bus driver in the city centre. We all live in a fairly basic house that my husband built for us. The house has one main room, where we work and eat, and two smaller rooms where we sleep. We also have a shower and toilet, which makes us the envy of the neighbourhood. We haven't got much in the way of possessions, but we do own a fridge and an old television set. We are lucky to have electricity here. The four older children all go out to work, to bring in some more money for the family. Pedro, who is 11, has just started shoe-shining in the city centre. He fits it in when he is not at school, but I think he will soon have to leave school and work full-time. We have been in Sao Paulo for 15 years now. Each year we manage to improve our standard of living very slightly. Maybe one day we'll be able to move out of here.'

Figure 4

Activities

1 Copy the map of Brazil in Figure 3. Use your atlas to label the following:

Major cities

Rio de Janeiro	Porto Alegre
Sao Paulo	Salvador
Brasilia	Recife
Belem	Fortaleza
Belo Horizonte	Manaus

Ocean

Atlantic Ocean

2 Name the ten countries that share a border with Brazil (see page 94).

3 Estimate how many times bigger Brazil is than Great Britain: 10 times, 35 times, or 60 times?

4 Isobella and Maria (Figure 4) lead very different lives. Isobella's family is quite well off, and Maria's family is quite poor. There are many people in Brazil who have a standard of living that is far higher than Isobella's or far lower than Maria's. Write about the main differences between the lives of Isobella and Maria.

3 Brazil: environmental contrasts

Brazil is a land of contrasts. It has some of the richest natural resources in the world. However, the country also experiences natural disasters such as drought, floods, and landslides. The industrial progress Brazil has experienced over the last twenty-five years has been based on the exploitation of the natural resources that have been discovered. Some parts of Brazil remain almost unexplored, so the real natural wealth of the country is not yet fully known.

Figure 1 Brazil's natural resources

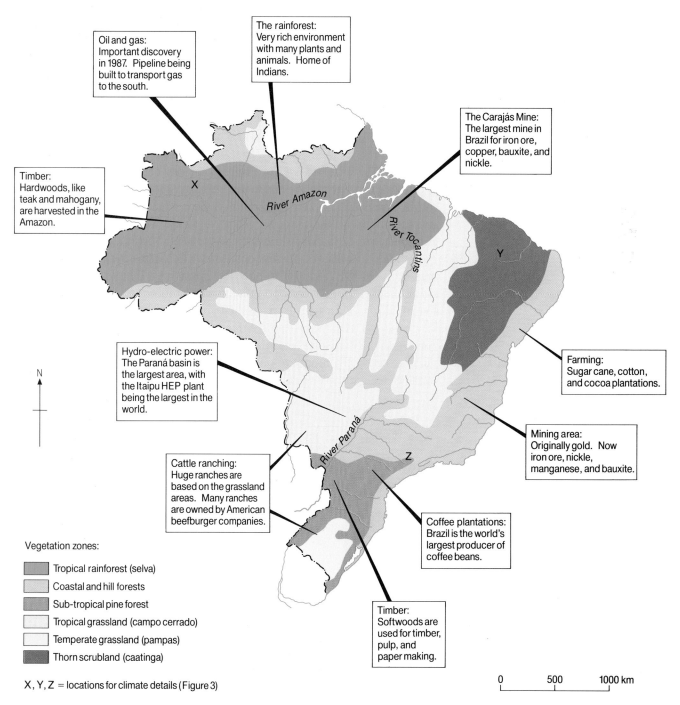

Oil and gas:
Important discovery in 1987. Pipeline being built to transport gas to the south.

The rainforest:
Very rich environment with many plants and animals. Home of Indians.

The Carajás Mine:
The largest mine in Brazil for iron ore, copper, bauxite, and nickle.

Timber:
Hardwoods, like teak and mahogany, are harvested in the Amazon.

River Amazon

River Tocantins

X

Y

Hydro-electric power:
The Paraná basin is the largest area, with the Itaipu HEP plant being the largest in the world.

Farming:
Sugar cane, cotton, and cocoa plantations.

River Paraná

Z

Mining area:
Originally gold. Now iron ore, nickle, manganese, and bauxite.

Cattle ranching:
Huge ranches are based on the grassland areas. Many ranches are owned by American beefburger companies.

Coffee plantations:
Brazil is the world's largest producer of coffee beans.

N

Vegetation zones:

- Tropical rainforest (selva)
- Coastal and hill forests
- Sub-tropical pine forest
- Tropical grassland (campo cerrado)
- Temperate grassland (pampas)
- Thorn scrubland (caatinga)

Timber:
Softwoods are used for timber, pulp, and paper making.

X, Y, Z = locations for climate details (Figure 3)

0   500   1000 km

Climate is the most important factor affecting vegetation zones in Brazil. Although the country lies mainly in the tropics, it experiences a large range of climatic conditions.

The North has an equatorial climate where the weather is hot and humid all year round. These conditions are ideal for the rainforest.

The South experiences a temperate climate. Temperatures are seasonal, falling between May and September, rising to a peak in January and February. This is the opposite to Britain, because southern Brazil is in the southern hemisphere.

Figure 2 One type of vegetation in Brazil

Temperature (°C)	J	F	M	A	M	J	J	A	S	O	N	D	Mean
Sao Gabriel	25	26	26	25	25	25	24	25	25	26	26	26	25
Quixeramobin	29	28	27	27	27	26	27	28	28	29	29	29	28
Sao Paulo	21	21	21	19	17	15	15	16	16	18	19	20	18
Rainfall mm	J	F	M	A	M	J	J	A	S	O	N	D	Total
Sao Gabriel	269	222	261	247	305	232	227	207	151	166	194	303	2784
Quixeramobin	42	121	209	173	118	58	16	5	6	3	4	10	765
Sao Paulo	215	175	161	77	65	40	24	48	92	121	138	188	1344

Figure 3 Climate data for X, Y, and Z in Figure 1

Activities

1 Match up the photograph of vegetation in Figure 2 with the correct vegetation zone on the map.

2 Look at the map in Figure 1. Make a list of Brazil's main natural resources.

3 a) Using the data in Figure 3, draw climate graphs for Sao Gabriel, Quixeramobin, and Sao Paulo.
b) What are the main differences in the climate between the three places?
c) Which place experiences an equatorial climate?
d) Which place is likely to experience drought?

4 Brazil: economic contrasts

In just twenty-five years, between 1960 and 1985, Brazil changed from being a poor country to the ninth-wealthiest country in the world. This rapid change makes us want to ask two important questions:

How did it happen?
Did everyone and every region of Brazil gain from this progress?

The 'Economic Miracle'

1964 Military goverment came to power in Brazil. The government started borrowing money from foreign banks to build large-scale projects such as dams and mines.

1964-73 Industrial output in the country doubled. This was the 'Economic Miracle'!

1973 Oil crisis. Brazil had to spend far more money on imports to buy the oil it needed. Government borrowed more money to buy the oil.

1979 Oil prices rose again. Foreign banks increased their interest charges, so Brazil owed more and more money.

1982 Brazil could not afford to pay back the loans. Industrial expansion stopped. Wages dropped, and many lost their jobs.

1985 Civilian government took power.

1989 Brazil owed $118 billion to foreign banks. Imports were cut drastically to try and save money.

Figure 1

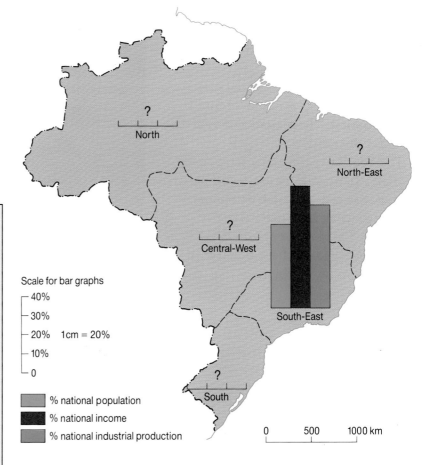

Scale for bar graphs
- 40%
- 30%   1cm = 20%
- 20%
- 10%
- 0

▢ % national population
■ % national income
▢ % national industrial production

0   500   1000 km

Regions	% national population	% national income	% national industrial production
North	5	2	2
North-East	29	14	16
Central-West	6	3	5
South-East	44	64	55
South	16	17	22

Figure 2 Regional economic contrasts in Brazil. For use with Activities 2 and 3

Despite all the problems, Brazil has become one of the major industrial countries of the world. Industrialisation has brought wealth to the country, but it is not evenly spread amongst the regions, or the people.

Why are there regional differences? As you can see from the table in Figure 2, most of the country's industrial production is located in the South-East. The Fiat case study helps to explain why this is so.

Case Study: Fiat, Belo Horizonte

In 1978, Fiat, the Italian car company, opened a factory in Belo Horizonte, in the South-East of Brazil. The factory produces over 130 000 cars a year, and employs thousands of peole. Why did Fiat choose to come to Belo Horizonte?

While Brazil has become richer as a country, it is true to say that most people in Brazil have not benefited from the country's industrial growth. Many of the poor have in fact become poorer. Increases in taxes, high unemployment, and the rapidly rising cost of goods have taken away what little money the poor had.

The landowners and industrialists are the ones who have gained most from the industrial development. As you can see from Figure 4, in 1980 the wealthiest 20 per cent of the population in Brazil earned 66 per cent of the national earnings, whilst the poorest 20 per cent earned only 2 per cent.

The gap between the rich and the poor is rapidly widening.

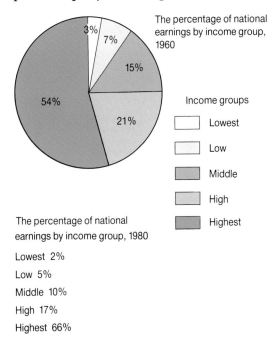

The percentage of national earnings by income group, 1960

Income groups
- Lowest
- Low
- Middle
- High
- Highest

The percentage of national earnings by income group, 1980

Lowest 2%
Low 5%
Middle 10%
High 17%
Highest 66%

Figure 4 The distribution of earnings in Brazil

Belo Horizonte - The Ideal Location

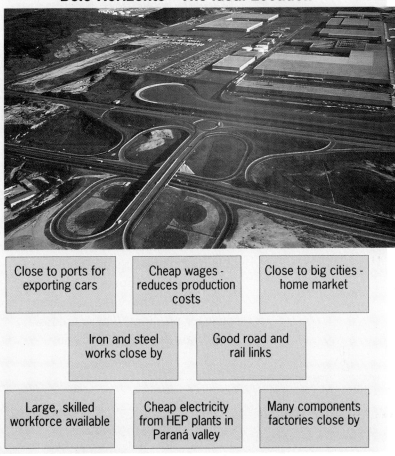

- Close to ports for exporting cars
- Cheap wages - reduces production costs
- Close to big cities - home market
- Iron and steel works close by
- Good road and rail links
- Large, skilled workforce available
- Cheap electricity from HEP plants in Paraná valley
- Many components factories close by

Figure 3 The advantages enjoyed by the Fiat car plant at Belo Horizonte

Activities

1 Why do you think that people talked about the 'Economic Miracle' in Brazil?

2 Draw a map to compare Brazil's regions. To do this copy the map in Figure 2 and complete it by drawing bar graphs for percentage (%) population, percentage (%) national income, and percentage (%) industrial production in each region. The information you will need is in the table (Figure 2).

3 Use your map to say which region is the least developed. Try and give a reason for this.

4 Why did Fiat not choose to locate their factory in the North?

5 a) Use the table in Figure 4 to draw a pie chart showing the distribution of national earnings in 1980.
b) Compare the two pie charts. Which income groups are better off and which are worse off?
c) Working in groups or on your own, decide what might be done to stop the gap between the rich and the poor getting wider.

5 Brazil: trading partners

Figure 1 The trade marks of some large foreign companies which have built factories in Brazil

Brazil's progress towards development depends on how successfully the country can sell the goods it produces to other countries. The companies above are all involved in producing goods for export from Brazil. The map (Figure 2) shows the main places to which these products are exported.

Forty per cent of Brazil's exports are primary products. These are raw materials that have not been processed. The main ones are coffee beans, sugar cane, cocoa beans, iron ore, beef, and soya beans.

More money can be made from exporting manufactured goods, such as cars, clothes, and shoes. These now account for 60 per cent of Brazil's exports.

Brazil also needs to import a large range of goods from other countries. These include crude petroleum,

The main sources of Brazil's imports	
USA	23%
EC	23%
South America	13%
Middle East and Africa	17%
Japan	6%

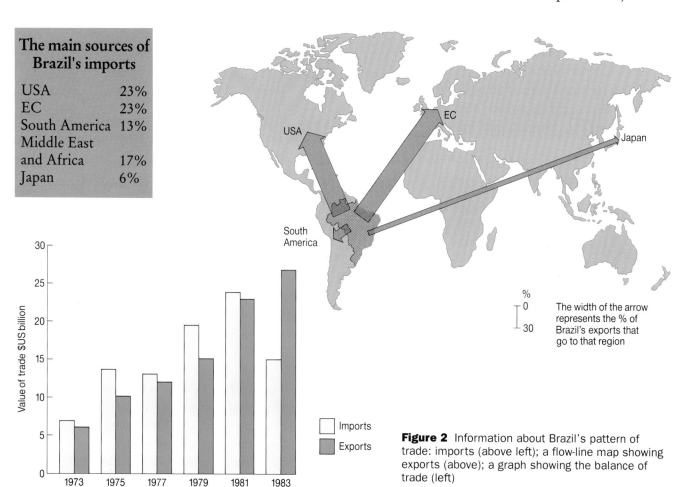

The width of the arrow represents the % of Brazil's exports that go to that region

Figure 2 Information about Brazil's pattern of trade: imports (above left); a flow-line map showing exports (above); a graph showing the balance of trade (left)

machinery, chemicals, and cereal products. The sources of these imports are shown in Figure 2.

Brazil is the world's largest coffee producer. Twenty years ago coffee made up 30 per cent of all of Brazil's exports. Today it accounts for less than 10 per cent, but it is still an essential part of Brazil's economy.

Most of Brazil's coffee is exported in the form of coffee beans. The coffee beans are usually processed by the country which imports the beans. The coffee growers in Brazil only get about 37p out of every 100p spent on jars of coffee in the shops. The rest of the money goes to countries like Britain, where the beans are processed and sold.

Activities

1 Using a world map outline and the data in Figure 2, draw a flow-line map of where Brazil's imports come from. Use the same scale as the map for exports in Figure 2.

2 Compare your flow-line map for imports with the map for exports. List the countries which sell more to Brazil than Brazil sells to them.

3 Look at Brazil's balance of trade (the graph in Figure 2).
a) In which year was there the biggest trade deficit (larger imports than exports)?
b) When was a trade surplus first recorded (larger exports than imports)?

4 Read about the coffee industry in Brazil.
a) Draw a pie chart to show where the money goes (see Figure 3).
b) Do you think the distribution of money is fair? If not, how do you think the money should be distributed?

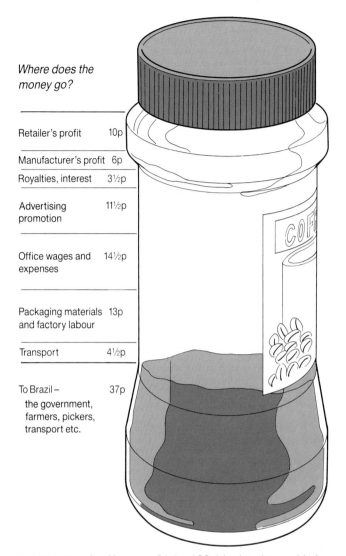

Where does the money go?

Retailer's profit	10p
Manufacturer's profit	6p
Royalties, interest	3½p
Advertising promotion	11½p
Office wages and expenses	14½p
Packaging materials and factory labour	13p
Transport	4½p
To Brazil – the government, farmers, pickers, transport etc.	37p

Figure 3 If this jar of coffee cost £1 (or 100p) in the shops, this is roughly where the money would go

Figure 4 Sacks of coffee beans being loaded onto a ship at Santos. This ship was bound for Germany

6 Global interdependence

The cartoon in Figure 1 shows that we all live in the same world and rely on each other for our survival. The wealthy countries of the North need the resources from the countries of the South. The poorer countries of the South can benefit from the technology of the North to exploit these resources, and to develop their own industries. This link is known as interdependence. The idea of global interdependence was highlighted by 'The Brandt Commission' in the 1980 report called 'North-South - A Programme for Survival'. The message of the report was that developed and developing countries have to act together to resolve their differences and face common threats such as famine and exhaustion of resources. The gap between the rich and poor countries should be closed.

Has the relationship between the rich and poor countries of the world improved since the Brandt Report? The cartoon in Figure 2 suggests that we do not live in an equal world.

Trade links tend to favour developed countries. The game opposite shows many of the situations that rich and poor countries face when dealing with each other.

Figure 1 The caption for this cartoon was 'We're all in the same boat'

Figure 2 What would be a suitable caption for this cartoon?

One of the ways in which rich countries can help poor countries is to give aid. There are three main sources of aid:
1. Bilateral aid. This goes directly from one country to another. It could be in the form of grants, loans, advice from scientists, or education for students from poor countries in the donor country.
2. Multilateral aid. This is aid from international organisations such as UNICEF, the World Bank, and the EC Development Fund. The money usually finances specific projects such as irrigation schemes or health clinics.
3. Charities. Aid is given by voluntary organisations, such as Oxfam and Christian Aid, to poor countries. Money is raised through fund raising activities, collections, and charity shops. It is mainly used for small-scale projects and disaster relief.

However, most of the aid given to the poor country will be used to buy goods from the donor country.

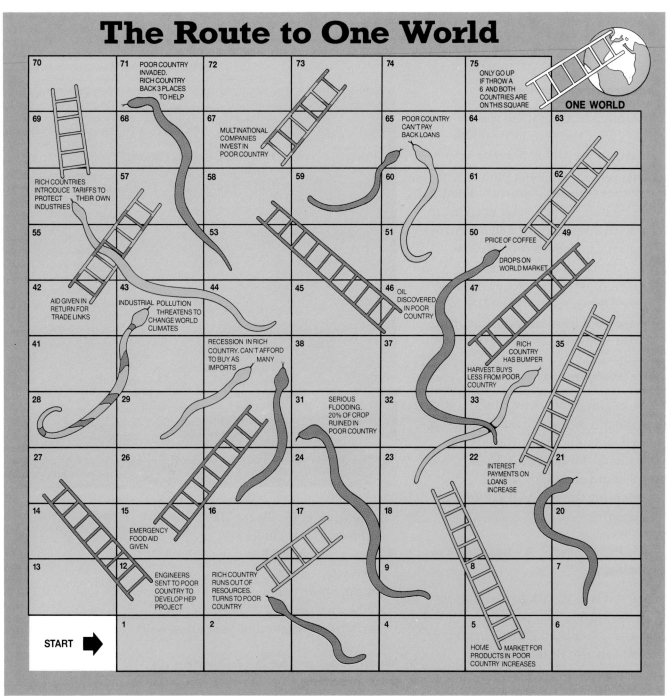

The Route to One World

70	71 POOR COUNTRY INVADED. RICH COUNTRY BACK 3 PLACES TO HELP	72	73	74	75 ONLY GO UP IF THROW A 6 AND BOTH COUNTRIES ARE ON THIS SQUARE **ONE WORLD**
69	68	67 MULTINATIONAL COMPANIES INVEST IN POOR COUNTRY	65 POOR COUNTRY CAN'T PAY BACK LOANS	64	63
RICH COUNTRIES INTRODUCE TARIFFS TO PROTECT THEIR OWN INDUSTRIES	57	58	59	60	61	62
55	53	51	50 PRICE OF COFFEE	49
42 AID GIVEN IN RETURN FOR TRADE LINKS	43 INDUSTRIAL POLLUTION THREATENS TO CHANGE WORLD CLIMATES	44	45	46 OIL DISCOVERED IN POOR COUNTRY	47 DROPS ON WORLD MARKET
41	RECESSION IN RICH COUNTRY. CAN'T AFFORD TO BUY AS MANY IMPORTS	38	37	35 RICH COUNTRY HAS BUMPER HARVEST. BUYS LESS FROM POOR COUNTRY
28	29	31 SERIOUS FLOODING. 20% OF CROP RUINED IN POOR COUNTRY	32	33
27	26	24	23	22 INTEREST PAYMENTS ON LOANS INCREASE	21
14	15 EMERGENCY FOOD AID GIVEN	16	17	18	20
13	12 ENGINEERS SENT TO POOR COUNTRY TO DEVELOP HEP PROJECT	RICH COUNTRY RUNS OUT OF RESOURCES. TURNS TO POOR COUNTRY	9	8	7
START ➡	1	2	4	5	6 HOME MARKET FOR PRODUCTS IN POOR COUNTRY INCREASES

How to play: You will need two counters, a dice, and two players. One player is representing a rich country (blue) and the other a poor country (red). Both players need to throw a six to start. Blue snakes and ladders are to be used by the rich country. Red snakes and ladders are to be used by the poor country. Multicoloured snakes and ladders are to be used by both rich and poor countries. The aim of the game is for both countries to reach 'One World'.

Figure 3

Activities

1 Play the snakes and ladders game to see if you can reach 'One World'.
a) Record the events that happen.
b) Is the game like the real world? Explain your answer.

2 Look at the two cartoons.
a) Explain in detail what they are trying to say.
b) Think of a suitable caption for the cartoon in Figure 2.

3 What is meant by 'global interdependence'?

4 Why do you think rich countries give aid to poor countries? Make a list of five possible reasons.

7 Assignment: Allocating UN funds

Background information

The United Nations (UN) was set up in 1945 after the Second World War. The aim of the UN is to try to keep world peace by reducing the likelihood of conflict between countries. The UN takes on many tasks, such as trying to help with disaster relief and improving education and health care. Nearly every country in the world is a member. Most of the money used to run the UN, or spent by the UN in the world, comes from the richer countries who are members.

Your assignment

Work in groups of six for this assignment. You are to hold a meeting of the UN to discuss how to spend your money for next year. Each member of your group will be representing the views of a different UN country.

Work Programme A - holding the meeting

What you will be talking about at the meeting (the agenda) is shown opposite. Details on each item on the agenda can also be found on the opposite page.

● You will need to elect a chairperson who will organise the meeting. You will also need to decide, before you start, how decisions on each item are going to be made.

● A record of the meeting (called minutes) should be kept by all group members.

● Each member of the group needs to represent one of the following

Figure 1 The UN General Assembly

countries: USA, Brazil, UK, Ethiopia, Japan, India.

● You will need to do some research about your country before you can begin. Study the quality of life indicators on page 79. You may find further information in your atlas.

Work Programme B - following up your meeting

● Write up the minutes of the meeting, including the decisions that were made, and each country's views on these decisions.

● Draw a bar graph to show your planned expenditure.

● What else do you think the UN should be spending money on?

● What are your personal views on your group's decisions?

Figure 2 The UN symbol

UNITED NATIONS AGENDA

Item 1: Income (Annual contributions)
Items 2-7: Expenditure
Item 2: UN Defence Force
Item 3: Health Care
Item 4: Food Aid
Item 5: Agricultural Improvements
Item 6: Industrial Development
Item 7: Large-Scale Development Projects

ITEMS 2 - 7 : EXPENDITURE

Once you have decided how much money you have available to spend, your group can decide how they wish to spend the money.
There are six items on the agenda that you are allowed to spend money on. You do not have to spend money on each item, but you must be able to justify your decisions. You cannot overspend.

ITEM 2 : UN DEFENCE FORCE

OPTION 1 To establish a powerful international army, navy, and airforce that could intervene in any international conflicts.
COST: $25 000 million a year.
OPTION 2 To establish a small neutral international army that could back up other countries defence forces, if a conflict arose.
COST: $5000 million a year.

ITEM 3 : HEALTH CARE

OPTION 1 To set up primary health care facilities in all developing countries. The health facilities should aim at preventing health problems through vaccination and health education. There should be many small-scale centres, so that they may be easily reached by the people who need to use the facilities.
COST: $10 000 million.
OPTION 2 To build one large hospital in every developing country. The hospital would be well equipped to treat all likely diseases and health problems.
COST: $15 000 million.
OPTION 3 To set up a training programme in developing countries, to train local people to become doctors and nurses.
COST: $8000 million.

ITEM 4 : FOOD AID

OPTION 1 To establish an emergency food fund to deal with any famines that may happen in the next year.
COST: $10 000 million.

ITEM 1 : INCOME (ANNUAL CONTRIBUTIONS)

The UN raises funds by donations from member countries. It is expected that wealthier members should give more money.
There are three options for the following year:
OPTION 1 Each country with a GDP per capita greater than $2500 contributes 0.1% of its annual GDP to the UN.
This would raise $8000 million.
OPTION 2 Each country with a GDP per capita greater than $2500 contributes 0.5% of its annual GDP to the UN.
This would raise $40 000 million.
OPTION 3 Each country with a GDP per capita greater than $2500 contributes 1.0% of its annual GDP to the UN.
This would raise $80 000 million.

ITEM 5 : AGRICULTURAL IMPROVEMENTS

OPTION 1 Establish a research institute to develop high yield crop varieties that can be used in developing countries. These crops will need pesticides and fertilisers for them to be successful.
COST: $7000 million.
OPTION 2 Send modern agricultural machinery, such as tractors and combine harvesters, to developing countries.
COST: $15 000 million.
OPTION 3 Send engineers and agriculturalists to developing countries to work with local people to develop appropriate solutions to their individual farming problems. This may involve developing a simple irrigation scheme, improving a well, or making equipment from local resources to use on the land.
COST: $8000 million.

ITEM 6 : INDUSTRIAL DEVELOPMENT

OPTION 1 Send the necessary machinery to developing countries to allow them to process some of their own natural resources. For example, to make jars of instant coffee from coffee beans.
COST: $15 000 million.
OPTION 2 Encourage multinational companies to invest in developing countries by giving them incentives. Cars, clothes, and so on can be made cheaply in developing countries, and jobs are provided for local people. Most of the profits are kept by the multinational company.
COST: $5000 million.

ITEM 7 : LARGE-SCALE DEVELOPMENT PROJECTS

OPTION 1 Provide some money and expertise towards the building of a major development project in each developing country.
COST: $20 000 million.

— international boundary

• capital city

abbreviations:

AUST.	AUSTRIA
B	BOSNIA-HERZEGOVINA
BELG.	BELGIUM
C	CROATIA
CENT. AF. REP.	CENTRAL AFRICAN REPUBLIC
CZECH.	CZECHOSLOVAKIA
L	LIECHTENSTEIN
LUX.	LUXEMBOURG
NETH.	NETHERLANDS
S	SLOVENIA
SWITZ.	SWITZERLAND
U.A.E.	UNITED ARAB EMIRATES
U.S.A.	UNITED STATES OF AMERICA

Modified Gall Projection

GREENLAND
(Den.)

• Godthåb
(Nuuk)

Alaska
(USA)

C A N A D A

U. S. A.

• Washington
D.C.

Azores
(Port.)

Bermuda
(U.K.)

Hawaiian Is.
(USA)

Nassau •
THE
BAHAMAS

Havana • CUBA

MEXICO

Mexico •

JAMAICA

HAITI

DOMINICAN
REPUBLIC

ST. KITTS-NEVIS

CAPE VERDE

Belmopan •
BELIZE

Kingston •

Puerto
Rico
(U.S.A.)

DOMINICA

GUATEMALA

Guatemala •

HONDURAS

ST. LUCIA
ST. VINCENT

BARBADOS

San Salvador • Tegucigalpa

GRENADA

EL SALVADOR

NICARAGUA

TRINIDAD AND
TOBAGO

Managua •

San José •

Caracas •

COSTA RICA

Panamá •

VENEZUELA

GUYANA

PANAMA

Bogotá •

Georgetown • Paramaribo •

SURINAM

Cayenne •

FRENCH GUIANA

COLOMBIA

Galapagos
Is. (Ec.)

Quito •

ECUADOR

B R A Z I L

P
E
R
U

Lima •

Brasilia •

• La Paz

BOLIVIA

PARAGUAY

Asuncion •

C
H
I
L
E

ARGENTINA

URUGUAY

Santiago •

Buenos
Aires •

Montevideo •

Falkland Is. (U.K.)

• Stanley

South Georgia
(U.K.)

Antarctica

A world map like this cannot show
Antarctica accurately.
Antarctica requires a separate map.

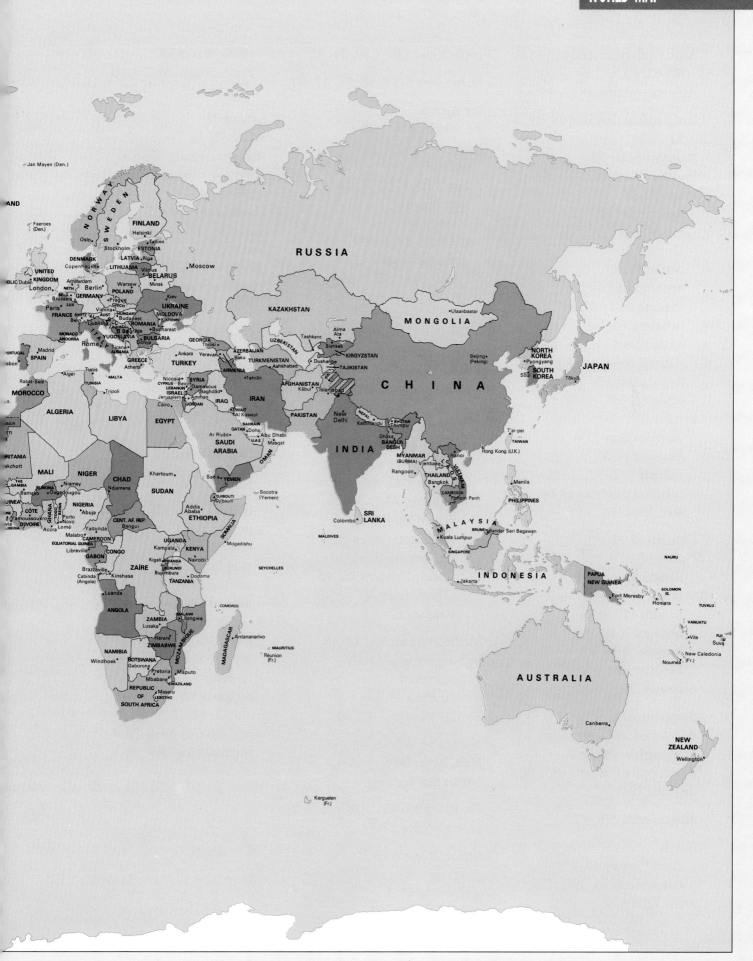